Letter from the Editors

Welcome to 2017, everyone! We've lost a few hundred subscribers as the year ticked over, which was a little unexpected. If you're still reading, thanks for sticking around. We have to change plans slightly because of this. We wanted to increase page count and possibly move to six issues a year, but that will now have to wait.

We still have a jam-packed issue for you! First up is a long feature on the house made famous by "Downton Abbey", Highclere Castle - which we had the pleasure of visiting last year. We've also got a lovely assortment of articles about The WI, The Spitfire, Alfred the Great, and The Yankee Invasion of Britain during World War II. Laurence returns again with a new article in Lost in the Pond, and Erin Moore is back with a great article about how she ended up living the Anglophile dream in Britain.

Even in the dead of winter, England is still an incredibly beautiful place. The grass stays green year round in Britain, so even on a cold winter's day, you can enjoy the lovely scenery offered up by the English countryside. Winter flowers such as the snowdrops appear, and in February, daffodils start to bloom. And before you know it, it's springtime in England; quite possibly the most beautiful time of year.

We hope you enjoy this issue and we can't wait to share more of our adventures with you.

Cheers,
Jonathan & Jackie
Publishers
Anglotopia

Table of Contents

Finding Downton..2
Poem..12
Then & Now...14
Song..16
The Women's Institute.......................................18
Lost in the Pond..22
Alfred the Great..24
10 Worst Britons in History.............................28
Great British Art...32
Great British Icons: The Spitfire......................34
This English Life...38
Q&A..41
The Yankee Invasion..42
Brit Book Corner..48
Great Britons: William Herschel.....................50
Northern Renaissance: Hull.............................54
London Uncovered...58
The Slang Page..64

About the Magazine

The Anglotopia Magazine is published quarterly by Anglotopia LLC, a USA registered Corporation. All contents copyrighted and may not be reproduced without permission.

Letters to the Editors may be addressed to:

Anglotopia LLC
1101 Cumberland Crossing #120
Valparaiso, IN 46383
USA

Photos: Cover: Highclere Castle. Back cover: Cottage Row, Shaftesbury. Inside Back Cover: Rainy Weymouth, Dorset

FINDING DOWNTON

Our Journey to Highclere Castle

By Jonathan Thomas

Only a few places in Britain become part of the global popular imagination, and Highclere Castle is one of them. Many of you may remember it from Jeeves and Wooster, its first claim to fame or as the home of Lord Carnarvon, who funded of the discovery of King Tut's Tomb. But now the whole world knows the house as Downton Abbey, the setting of the world's most popular costume drama that recently ended its run. We had the opportunity to visit this past spring; it was the journey of a lifetime.

Highclere: A Brief History

Even before the success of "Downton Abbey," if you possess a passion for grand English houses, then Highclere Castle should surely have been on your list of places to visit, at least once in your life. Located just south of Newbury in Berkshire, the house is actually located in the county of Hampshire. The estate extends to over 5,000 acres and is still the country home of the Earl of Carnarvon (though they only live in it part of the year).

The origins of the estate stretch back almost 1300 years. Highclere Castle is the fifth or sixth house to be built on the estate property. It was once a larger estate that was built by the Bishops of Winchester, which dates back to the 8th century. The original site was actually recorded in the Domesday Book (William the Conqueror's accounting of his newly conquered Kingdom). However, it was in 1679 when the home was taken into the hands of the Carnarvon family, who still own it today. As an aside, the house was called a house or perhaps even Abbey, then a Palace, then a Placehouse and now is called a Castle due to its grandeur; despite not looking much like a castle in the traditional sense.

During this period, it was a square, classical style mansion. In 1692, the estate was gifted as a wedding present by Robert Sawyer to his daughter, Margaret, who married the 8th Earl of Pembroke. The second son of Margaret, Robert Sawyer Herbert, went on to inherit Highclere and made his own impact on the estate by creating a formal garden with 12 temples and follies. His nephew and heir to the estate, Henry Herbert, later known as Baron Porchester, became the 1st Earl of Carnarvon thanks to George III.

It was in 1838 that the 3rd Earl commissioned Sir Charles Barry, the person responsible for the rebuilding of the Houses of Parliament. During this period, there was a Renaissance Revival movement, which Barry was greatly skilled at creating. However, at Highclere, he designed the estate with Jacobethan-style influences. There are touches of details that do reflect the Renaissance-based characteristics, such as the towers of the castle, which are slimmer than others built during the same period. It is said that when Barry was creating a rough draft of the house design, he used all Italian Renaissance characteristics. However, it was rejected by the Earl.

If you think it looks like the houses of Parliament, that's intentional. The Houses of Parliament, reconstructed after they burned down in 1834, were also designed by Barry, the pre-eminent Victorian architect. It is not a design style that thrived into the 20th century. In fact, many famous neo-gothic buildings were tragically pulled down as tastes changed and the maintenance costs skyrocketed.

The 3rd Earl died in 1849, and Sir Charles Barry died in 1860. At this time, the West Wing was still not completed; where the servants' quarters were designated to be located. The 4th Earl commissioned the services of architect Thomas Allom, who had worked with Barry in previous years, to help supervise the finished construction of the castle. It was finally completed in 1878 - quite a stretch of time from beginning to end. Many of Britain's great houses took generations to build and look like they do today - Highclere is no exception.

During the 20th century, Highclere Castle was the meeting place for all sorts of important people. Visitor books recorded that the house parties hosted at the castle were visited by Egyptologists, aviators, soldiers, technological innovators, and politicians. The 5th Countess of Carnarvon, Almina, transformed the house into a hospital during World War I to help soldiers coming home from the battles in Flanders, Belgium. Almina became a skilled nurse and healer which was chronicled in numerous letters found from patients and their families who thanked her for her generosity.

In 1919, the castle returned back into a private home for the 5th Earl of Carnarvon and his family. After his death in 1923, his son returned to Highclere Castle where he resided until 1986.

You may recognize the 7th Earl of Carnarvon from the recent Netflix drama "The Crown." Lord Porchester, or Porchie as he was known to the

The Current Lady of Carnarvon Relaxes in the Stunning Library

young Queen, was a close friend of Her Majesty. They both shared a passion for horses and worked together for many years breeding horses. Porchie went on to become the Queen's racing manager in 1969 and was known as one of the few people who could contact Her Majesty directly to speak about her beloved horses. "The Crown" speculates that there may have been more to their relationship, but we'll never really know. He was an important British statesman and local politician and became the 7th Earl of Carnarvon following the death of his father in 1987. Lord Porchester died on September 11th, 2001 (nothing to do with the other major event that happened that day).

The current residents of Highclere Castle are the 8th Earl and Countess of Carnarvon. Lord Carnarvon and his father opened the Castle to the public in 1988, and before "Downton Abbey," they had a very successful wedding business. Lord and Lady Carnarvon were living partly in the Castle since 2003 as they do today (they stay less in the Castle when it's open to the public). They created the Egyptian Exhibition in 2007 which was very successful and remains open today.

The estimated cost of the repairs was around £12 million (around $20 million) relating to the ancient barns and follies as well as to the Castle itself. They have always undertaken a steady programme of repairs, although, like with many country houses there was an investment deficit of repairs which had accumulated since World War II. Thanks to the increase in visitors since 2012 due to the success of Downton Abbey, the Earl and Lady Carnarvon could get on with their work at the Castle. The family lives in Highclere Castle during the winter months and then return to their cottage during the summer when the castle is open to the public.

Owning a great house like this is quite a challenge. Lord and Lady Carnarvon undertook major roof repairs in 2003. Since then they have accumulated a great list of many specialists whether it be for roofs, stonework, plumbing or electrics. These homes were built to construction standards that were very different in the Victorian age, and while they were built with stone to stand the test of time, many aspects of the house do last. They were so well built, but given the size, the bills are always significant and for some great houses, more than they can manage. Roofs are the most common problem - often made of lead or slate. A leaky roof

The Exquisite Oak Staircase

is cancer to a stately home; it leads to rot and mold growth in the house which weakens the structure. Their age also compounds the second major problem; finding the necessary skills needed to fix these problems. However, Lady Carnarvon has built up a list of skilled tradesmen and a great team. It does take time, but that is not a problem when you measure the life of a house in hundreds of years.

Then there is also the issue of the plumbing, electrical and other services being woefully outdated. Thankfully, Highclere has been able to keep things modernised under a programme in force since 2003. It costs a fortune to keep the buildings up to modern standards to make sure the lights and the heating still work. If you don't keep these things updated, you have a problem that has felled many of Britain's lost stately homes: fire. Thankfully, a fire has not visited Highclere.

Many people think that the owners of houses like this are very rich but the phrase 'house rich, cash poor' applies here. Estates like Highclere cost a lot of money to run and maintain and like any business employ hundreds of people. Many Earl's and Dukes struggle to keep their heads above water. Many don't and give up their houses - they either abandon them or gift them to the National Trust. So, to find a beautiful house like Highclere, still in the hands of the original owner is quite a treat.

The success of "Downton Abbey" catapulted Highclere Castle to fame as the owners struggled to keep the house in good repair. Created by Julian Fellowes, the television drama was first aired in the United Kingdom on 26 September 2010 and in the United States on 9 January 2011. The series is set in a fictional estate called Downton Abbey (Highclere Castle) located in Yorkshire and portrays the life of the Crawley family, including that of their servants. The show is set in the post-Edwardian era and depicts how the great events of history have lasting effects on people in aristocratic positions (the sinking of the Titanic and the loss of the Estate's heir sets the show in motion). The show was not expected to last past the first season, but it became a worldwide hit - cementing its position as one of the most popular British costume dramas ever.

Visitors now stream in from all over the world to visit Highclere Castle on the days of the year that it is open. Income from admissions has ensured the survival of the house and allowed the owners to invest in a multi-year programme of repairs and renovations. The future of the house is secure for generations to come to enjoy.

Finding Downton - Our Visit

We have tried for several years to visit Highclere Castle. It's only open on a select number days of the year, and they sell tickets six months or more in advance. As a result, available tickets always sell out. And while they may have a few tickets left each day they're open for walk-up visitors, if you're in the USA and you can't get tickets in advance, it's too risky to plan a trip around it (but they recommend emailing in advance to see if you can get in at the last minute).

We managed to get tickets to visit in April 2016 the previous autumn when tickets became available for the spring opening. With our tickets secure, we were content to plan a trip around our visit there. As we bought our tickets and counted down the days, we couldn't wait to visit. To prepare ourselves, we binged watched old episodes of "Downton Abbey" and researched the background of the house.

The day of our visit arrived, and we woke up early in anticipation. We were staying in a self-catering cottage about an hour away in Dorset, so we had breakfast and got in the car for a lovely morning drive through the English countryside to the house. The drive took a little longer than we planned. We foolishly thought that Apple Maps could find its way to one of the most famous houses in the world, but alas it directed us to the private entrance. A quick Google search on the side of the road in Berkshire taught us that almost all Sat-navs get it wrong and we got the correct postcode to the visitor's entrance. Always check a house's website for directions before you try to go there!

We didn't mind really, we love driving in the English countryside, and it was a particularly beautiful sunny and clear day. We had morning tickets (the organizers split the day into morning tickets and afternoon ticket groups), which meant we could enter the house as soon as it opened to the public at 10 am. As we drove into the lawn and the area marked for parking, we discovered we were not the only ones with the idea to turn up early. After we parked the car and had our tickets checked, we were let past the gates and marveled as we walked up the drive to Downton Abbey, just like they do on the TV show. Thanks to Britain's appreciation for history,

The Capability Brown Shaped Landscape

there is no sign of the modern era we inhabit as you make your way up the walk. It is exactly as it is on the show - and exactly as it would be 100 years ago. Truly remarkable.

There were quite a few people about - many taking their fair share of pictures of the beautiful house. What struck us as we approached was just how massive the house really is. The marketing for the show can give you the impression that the house is quite small - but as you approach it, you experience it on a true scale that you can never have imagined. The place is massive. There are 200-300 rooms - though only a few are open to the public. The house is almost as massive as the Houses of Parliament in London in scale. You will also notice that the house sits perfectly in its surroundings. Just the right amount of sunlight hits the place, and it's perfectly situated in the Capability Brown designed landscape. Even though it was early spring, the grass was bright green, the trees lovely as ever. We had good weather on the day and didn't even need our coats.

We did not have to wait in line for long, it was clear there were a lot of people who were visiting that day, but the owners know how to manage the crowds. It's such a surreal moment to pass through the doors into the entryway we've seen so many times on TV. It's like walking right into the TV show. You're first ushered into the Gothic entrance hallway. A red carpet leads you to probably the most famous room in the house, the magnificent double height saloon where you can see the beautiful vaulted ceiling and the balcony to the upper level of the house.

Next was probably my most favorite room, the sumptuous double library. Most fans would recognize this as the study/office of the Earl of Grantham. And the room looks much like it does on the TV. The beautiful mahogany carved room is filled with hundreds of beautiful books. As someone who loves books and prides himself in keeping a large library, it was quite a treat to see such a beautiful space. I could have spent all day there.

It's not hard to imagine the room back in the late 1800's, a fire roaring in the hearth, a group of aristocrats drinking and smoking; discussing the politics of the day. Worrying about their estates and their inheritances. Pondering the British Empire and its causes. It's almost like a genteel club in London, the kind you'd find on Pall Mall.

Each room we visited had a helpful guide to expound on any trivia about objects in the room.

The Drawing Room

There were plenty of pictures from "Downton Abbey" showing the actors in the settings we know so well.

The crowd was happy. An Australian quipped loudly "We traveled 10,000 miles to see this place."

I responded to the kind room attendant that, "we'd only come 4,000 miles."

It was worth every mile traveled!

There is no guided tour aspect when you visit the house – it's self-guided. There are room attendants who will give occasional trivia but they're mostly there to make sure you don't touch anything. Though there was plenty of gossip about a possible "Downton Abbey" movie, "Oh, of course, we couldn't say." There are usually packets in each room that explain the history of the room and the items in them, but with the way, you must keep moving through the house, how much time you have to gaze at the beautiful artworks depends on how many people are in the house with you. But it's not hard to find a quiet moment to admire something.

As the tour continues, you're led through many more beautiful and sumptuous rooms, many of which never appeared on the show for various reasons (sometimes the artifacts in the rooms are too delicate to risk filming or the rooms too small to get the equipment inside). So, it was quite a treat to see rooms you were not expecting to see. What really struck me about the house, was not so much the size of the place, but how intimate it felt on the inside. It very much felt like a home. It felt almost wrong to be tramping through it with a crowd to admire the personal affects of 1300 years of Lords and Earls.

I especially liked learning more about the various objects in the interior. On the show, the objects are basically window dressing. Lord Fellowes, the creator of the show, often remarked that they picked the house because they had all the dead people's paintings you would need. They serve as background in the show; they give it gravitas. But they're never really remarked upon (though occasionally an artifact will become a plot point). So, it's lovely to finally be able to get some historical background on the paintings and sculptures we've all come to know so well.

After you've seen all the rooms on the main level, you're led upstairs to see all the private bedrooms. This was fascinating as the show usually didn't use these rooms for filming (but they sometimes did), they were often built on sets to make filming easier (as the rooms are quite small

The Double Height Saloon

for filming equipment to fit). Only a fraction of the more than 50-80 rooms in the house are open for you to see. The self-guided tour finishes with the opportunity to climb down the famous and beautiful oak staircase, just as Lord Grantham would with his dog Isis. I felt quite a tingle as I climbed down those stairs. After that, you're led to the outside of the house at the back, where you can find the gift shop and cafe. We were sure to buy several Highclere-related souvenirs (though there's no actual Downton merchandise).

Unfortunately, there are no kitchens on the tour. The current kitchens manage the tea rooms so are not open to the public. The wine cellars were taken over by the Egyptian Exhibition (see sidebar), so don't expect to see Mrs. Patmore preparing dinner in the basement! After you've seen the house, you have all the time you want to have a wander around the beautiful grounds, designed by renowned landscape architect Capability Brown. There's plenty of follies and ruins to take plenty of nice pictures.

We get this question a lot - if you love "Downton Abbey" - should you visit Highclere Castle? Most certainly, yes you should. You will not regret it. Would a visit be helped by binging "Downton Abbey" before your visit? Yes, absolutely.

Other TV & Film Appearances

Other TV and film appearances that utilized the Castle include: "The Secret Garden" (1987); "Eyes Wide Shut" (1999); "The Four Feathers" (2002); John Legend's music video for 'Heaven Only Knows' (2006). It was also featured in the classic comedy series "Jeeves & Wooster" as Totleigh Towers. Highclere Castle also rents its facilities for small film units, and photography sessions, many of which are wedding events.

Further Research

The current Countess of Carnarvon is a prolific writer and has written several fascinating books about the history of Highclere Castle. Most notably *Lady Almina and the Real Downton Abbey: The Lost Legacy of Highclere Castle, Lady Catherine, the Earl, and the Real Downton Abbey*. She also has a new book coming out in spring 2017 called *At Home at*

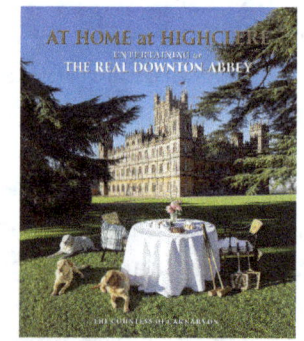

The Earl and King Tut

The 5th Earl of Carnarvon discovered a tomb which contained the Egyptian Boy Pharaoh, Tutankhamun, during an archaeological dig in 1922 with the help of his colleague, Howard Carter. They both spent 16 years working together through various excavation trips in Egypt. The Earl also helped Carter build a house in the desert close to the Valley of the Kings, which was properly nicknamed 'Castle Carter.' Both men were convinced that there were more tombs located in the Valley of the Kings. To help prove their hypothesis, they created a grid system in order to document where they had already excavated.

In the autumn of 1922, they planned one last excursion, in which the Earl's daughter, Lady Evelyn, also accompanied the men. Their trip was obviously a success due to the discovery of the Egyptian Boy Pharaoh. After the death of the 5th Earl, his widow sold his collection to the Metropolitan Museum, in New York, in order to pay for death duties. However, not all artifacts had been sold, and instead were tucked away in cupboards until they were re-

discovered by the Carnarvon family in 1987.

To help celebrate the success of the 5th Earl's accomplishment, the current Earl and Countess opened an Egyptian Exhibition in the cellars of the Castle, which is still present. This is also referred to as the 'Discovery Gallery,' which highlights different events that occurred for the Carnarvon family during the Great War, unfortunate financial situations, and the overall discovery of the Egyptian artifacts. The story was recently dramatised by ITV in a four part drama in 2016.

Highclere – Entertaining at The Real Downton Abbey, historic weekends, menus, and recipes. She also keeps a lovely blog at http://www.ladycarnarvon.com.

PBS also produced an excellent documentary about Highclere called "The Secrets of Highclere Castle" which is available on DVD and Blu-ray. It's also streaming via PBS and Amazon Prime.

Visiting Information

Highclere Castle is open for approximately 70 days each year. It is open for two weeks during the Easter holiday, May Bank holidays, and for a duration of two months during the summer, Sunday through to Thursday. It is also open for a few days in December to celebrate the Christmas holidays. There are guides in the rooms of the castle to answer any questions or gossip about Downton. They offer various discounted rates for large groups and school visits. Refer to the website for complete information about planning your visit: www.highclerecastle.co.uk. Tickets must be booked in advance and often sell out months ahead of time so planning ahead is critical. They also now have a yearly garden party with a theme where you're encouraged to dress up, 2017's will have a 1920s theme.

Ticket prices vary (and change yearly) but currently it's £22 (about $30) for an adult to visit the Castle, Egyptian Exhibition and Gardens, £13.50 (about $15) for Children, £60 (about $80) for a family of 4. Tickets are cheaper if you opt out of the Egyptian Exhibition (if you're not interested in Ancient Egypt, don't pay for it).

Special Note: No photography of any kind is allowed in the house!

Getting There

The house is relatively close to London. There are tour companies that can take you. But the best way to get there is to drive yourself. According to their website: "Please do not use a "sat nav" when close to Highclere Castle as this will bring you to the wrong entrance. If you do use the postcode RG20 9LE which is for a local restaurant, from there please follow the brown tourist signs to the main entrance."

You can also take a train directly from London Paddington to Newbury, where you can get a taxi to the house. This will cost between £15-20 each way (don't forget to book your return with the driver!). You can also take a bus from London Victoria to Newbury and take a taxi from there. Expect to spend 3-4 hours exploring the house and grounds.

As always, be sure to check Highclere's website (http://www.highclerecastle.co.uk) before visiting to make sure you have all the latest travel and opening information.

THE DARKLING THRUSH
By Thomas Hardy

I leant upon a coppice gate
    When Frost was spectre-grey,
And Winter's dregs made desolate
    The weakening eye of day.
The tangled bine-stems scored the sky
    Like strings of broken lyres,
And all mankind that haunted nigh
    Had sought their household fires.

The land's sharp features seemed to be
    The Century's corpse outleant,
His crypt the cloudy canopy,
    The wind his death-lament.
The ancient pulse of germ and birth
    Was shrunken hard and dry,
And every spirit upon earth
    Seemed fervourless as I.

At once a voice arose among
    The bleak twigs overhead
In a full-hearted evensong
    Of joy illimited;
An aged thrush, frail, gaunt, and small,
    In blast-beruffled plume,
Had chosen thus to fling his soul
    Upon the growing gloom.

So little cause for carolings
    Of such ecstatic sound
Was written on terrestrial things
    Afar or nigh around,
That I could think there trembled through
    His happy good-night air
Some blessed Hope, whereof he knew
    And I was unaware.

THEN

This is one of the earliest photos of the London Underground, taken in the 1890's when the Tube was already several decades old. You can tell that it already has a time-worn patina about it. This view of Marble Arch Tube Station is moody and atmospheric for everything that it shows. You can see that ads adorning the walls were with the Tube from the beginning. The platform is clearly made of wood, the benches classic benches you would find in a park. Both gentlemen look like just that - gentlemen.

NOW

This is Marble Arch taken fairly recently. Much has changed, but much is also very much the same. The tiles on the walls appear to be the same, while all the design details reflect a later time. There are still ads on the walls, though they're much bigger than they were in the past. The seats are a more uncomfortable metal type. It also appears to be much more brightly lit. The addition of the electronic sign at the top to announce the next train, is a nice addition. The floor is no longer made of wood but of tile, made to last much longer than wood ever would with the amount of traffic that goes through the Tube.

THERE'LL ALWAYS BE AN ENGLAND

There'll always be an England,
While there's a country lane,
Wherever there's a cottage small
Beside a field of grain.

There'll always be an England,
While there's a busy street,
Wherever there's a turning wheel
A million marching feet.

Red, white and blue,
What does it mean to you?
Surely you're proud
Shout it aloud.

Britons awake!
The Empire too,
We can depend on you,
Freedom remains
These are the chains
Nothing can break.

There'll always be an England,
And England shall be free,
If England means as much to you
As England means to me.

"This royal throne of kings, this sceptred isle,
This earth of majesty, this seat of Mars,
This other Eden, demi-paradise,
This fortress built by Nature for herself
Against infection and the hand of war,
This happy breed of men, this little world,
This precious stone set in a silver sea,
Which serves it in the office of a wall,
Or as a moat defensive to a house
Against the envy of less happier lands
This blessed plot, this earth, this realm
This England"

The Seven Sisters White Limestone Cliffs

© Peter Cripps / AdobeStock

AND WE WILL BUILD JERUSALEM

A History of the Women's Institute

Famous for country bake-sales and jam making, the Women's Institute was imported to Britain from Canada in 1915, to encourage farmers' wives to grow and preserve food for the war effort. It spread quickly and became a meeting place for country women in particular. Because each local group is independent, they can develop activities to meet local needs, but there is national unity too, with the National Federation of Women's Institutes, founded in 1917. Local WIs became institutions in almost every small town and community across the country, and have evolved as British society has evolved, always reflecting the needs of ordinary women and connecting them through practical activities and education.

On 16 September 1915, in a small single-storey building, with corrugated iron walls, nestled behind a rural stone wall, a group of local women gathered together. The gathering took place in the Welsh village of Llanfairpwllgwyngyll, also called Llanfair PG, a community of Welsh speakers, on the Isle of Anglesey. The meeting was organised by a Canadian called Madge Watts and an Englishman called John Nugent Harris.

Harris was secretary of the Agricultural Organisations Society (AOS), which had been formed in 1910 to promote the formation of agricultural cooperatives. These non-profit organisations were an off-shoot of the Socialist movement and brought farmers together to pool their resources to buy seed, supplies, and equipment, as well as to develop marketing outlets. In the growth of industry during the 19th century, agriculture had been left behind, many rural communities were poor, and the many tenant farmers, in particular, had very limited resources and powers. The AOS wanted to change all that, and in the suffragette atmosphere of the time, Harris was also keen to involve the wives as well as the farmers in his movement.

His inspiration came when he met Madge Watts, under unrecorded circumstances. She was from British Columbia but was in England because she had moved there, following the death of her husband, for the education of her two sons. Watts was a disciple of Adelaide Hoodless, who was born on a farm in Ontario. When a young mother, Hoodless had lost a child to illness exacerbated by drinking unpasteurised milk, an unhealthy but common practise at the time. She joined the YWCA to promote healthier practises in the home and went on to pioneer the teaching of domestic science to young girls in schools.

Following a speech in Stoney Creek, Ontario, to the local Farmer's Institute Ladies Night, Hoodless formed a women's group to promote education for farm women in domestic science and agriculture, as well as to provide a social gathering. These Women's Institutes spread rapidly across Ontario and then across Canada, and Madge Watts had been a founding member of the British Columbia Women's Institute, before moving to Britain. She was anxious to start Women's Institutes in Britain, and after meeting John Harris, the AOS hired her for six months to do just that.

Watts found a sponsor for that first meeting in Wales – the Marquis and Marchioness of Anglesey, whose land the farmers were tenants of. Tea and buttered bread were served, and, showing a frugality that would become a trademark of the WI, it was specified that just one kind of cake would be served. The combination of upper-class leadership and 'ordinary' members would characterise the WI, as well as give it respectability in a society where progress depended heavily on connections and class.

After the success of that first meeting, Madge Watts quickly founded new WI branches across the country. The initial focus was on growing and preserving food to help the war effort, and funding for the development of new branches was transferred from the OAS to the Food Department

Britain's Oldest WI Hall

Key Facts

- Began in 1915 in a village in Wales
- Directly developed from the original Canadian model
- A fixture in country communities for women of all ages and social classes
- Famous for their jumble-sales, baked goods, pickles, and especially for jam-making

of the Board of Agriculture. They paid for recruiters to spread out across the country so that by 1917 there were 137 separate WI branches. That year, joint meetings began to be held, leading to the formation of the National Federation of Women's Institutes.

The first Chairman of this new coordinating body was Baroness Gertrude Mary Denman, or Trudie, as she was known. A chain-smoking suffragette, Lady Denham had spent the war running the Smokes for Wounded Soldiers and Sailors Society, collecting 265 million cigarettes for the war effort. As head of the NFWI, she guarded its independence from the government, while still enjoying government funding. A dedicated eccentric, Lady Denham spearheaded campaigns ranging from sexual education (triggered by infected soldiers returning home after the war to pure wives), rabbit breeding, mobile libraries, and the quintessential jam-making, perhaps the badge of true WI membership. She held the post until 1946.

In 1948, the NFWI acquired Marsham Park, a 17th century Georgian home in what is today Oxfordshire. The house had once been the home of the famous 18th-century eccentric and miser John Elwes believed to be the inspiration for Ebenezer Scrooge in Charles Dickens' *A Christmas Carol*. The NFWO converted the house into a residential college and renamed it 'Denman College.' It continues to be an important part of the Women's Institute, running courses in everything from cooking and crafts to archaeology and researching your family tree.

The WI provided a place for women to meet, outside the home, and develop their own interests. Groups took part in self-education, first on domestic matters, but later on a wider range of activities. They

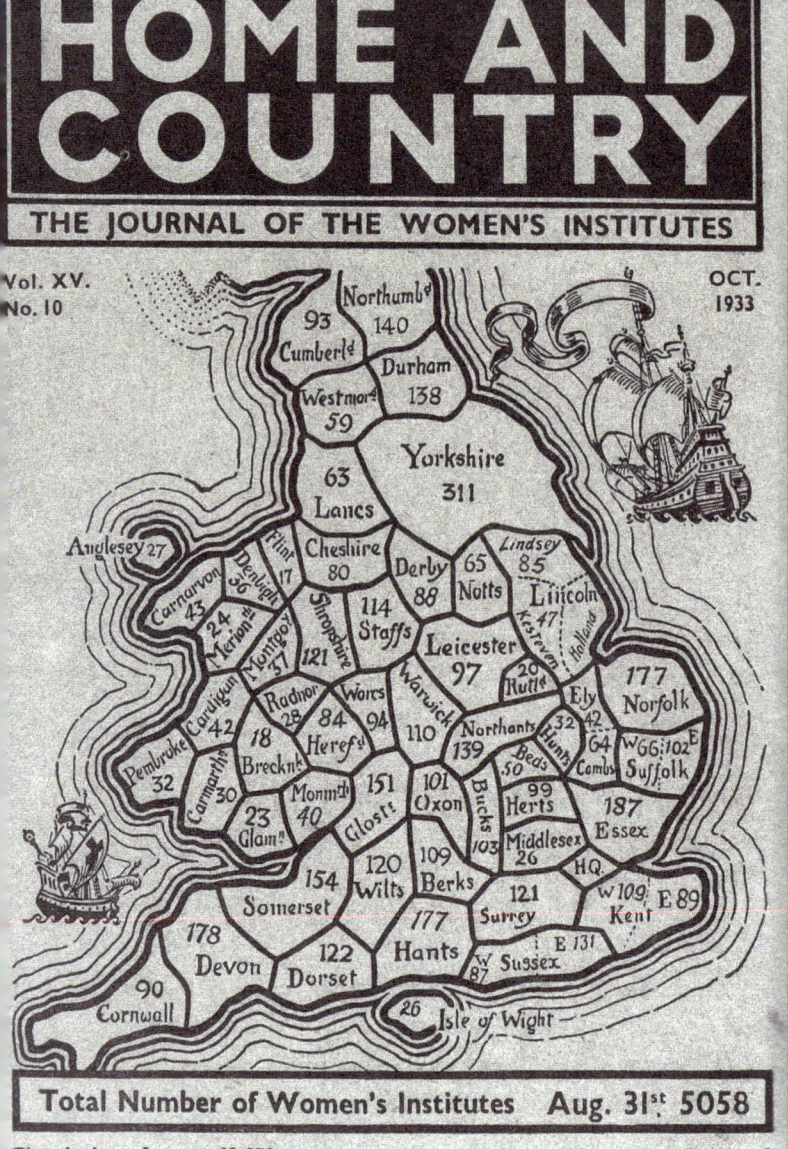

The WI Magazine from 1933

A WI During World War II was recently dramatised in Home Fires

carried out fund-raising, usually through jumble sales and selling homemade pickles and jams, as well as baked goods. An independent life outside the home was something new and novel, especially in the countryside, where there was little opportunity for women to become independent through employment, as there had been in cities.

Independence for women was not always welcomed. WI husbands called the institute "the curse of a married man's life" since a wife outside the home would not have supper ready on time. One village vicar imposed a curfew on women in his parish, forbidding them to go out after dark. Other critics considered enlightening women as pointless as attempting "to improve the condition of the beasts of the field."

In the 1960s, the 7th Marchioness of Anglesey followed in the footsteps of her husband's family and when just 29 became Chairman of the NFWI. During this period the number of Women's Institutes grew to almost nine thousand. The horizons of the WI expanded to include international issues, with the Freedom from Hunger Campaign raising money for Caribbean and South American causes.

With the growth of feminism in the 1970s younger country women were less likely to join the WI, and its demographic became older. Annual General Meetings passed resolutions condemning the availability of drugs and pornography to young people, but also expressed concern about marine pollution and the closing of village schools. When government regulations required that home kitchens selling food registered with local authorities, the NFWI successfully campaigned to have their jam-making members exempted from this regulation.

WI Ladies in their Sunday Best

But with the feisty independence of the typical WI member never far from sight, more radical actions have become prominent in recent decades. In 1999, 10 middle-aged Yorkshire WI members posed naked, with suitably-arranged cherry buns, for a calendar to raise money for leukaemia research. At the 2000 Annual Meeting the Prime Minister, Tony Blair, was slow hand-clapped during his speech, for delivering a political speech praising his contributions to the National Health Service, when in fact, he had made cuts and severely damaged the service.

What has made the WI so long-lived, and so successful, is that each group – and any group of women can start a new WI – can decide on what it wants to do. There is no national agenda to follow, so diversity rather than conformity is the theme, allowing each group to develop according to local needs and wishes, with their own local inspiration. Today there are 215,000 members in 6,300 Women's Institutes in the UK. The NFWI has become even more involved in political campaigning, for example with its current 'Care not Custody' campaign for improved treatment of the mentally ill.

Sites to Visit and Further Research

- Denman College is in the village of Marcham, Abingdon, Oxfordshire. The college offers day and residential courses in a variety of skills.
- NFWI headquarters is at 104 New Kings Road, London, SW6.

Further Research

- The Biography of the Women's Institutes can be read in: *A Force to Be Reckoned With*, by Jane Robinson (2011)
- The film *Calendar Girls* chronicles the midadventures of a Yorkshire based WI group who launched a nude calendar and became internationally famous. It's also been turned into a musical in London's West End.
- The recent PBS Masterpiece/ITV Production *Home Fires* dramatises the women of a Cheshire WI during World War II.

LOST IN THE POND
A British Expat's Guide to Cycling During a Chicago Winter
By Laurence Brown

There are three certainties in life: You are born; you die, and in between the British will always moan about the weather. But—as a Brit living in America—one of the first things I discovered upon my move here in 2008 is that British weather ain't got nothing on the American Midwest. And that particular revelation came to me while I was still living in Indiana; regular readers of this column, however, will note that the wife and I recently threw caution to the wind (literally, I suppose), and moved northwest to Chicago. And let me tell you about Chicago…

Chicago hangs immediately to the west of Lake Michigan, a body of water noted not only for its sheer size (it has a total surface area equal to four Northern Irelands) but for producing what is known locally as lake-effect snow. And, because of Chicago's relative proximity to Canada, the white stuff is accompanied by temperatures that are not entirely fit for humans.

For Brits like me, this is bad. Very, very bad. Not only does it make Britain feel like a fortnight in Tenerife, but it presents one or two (or eight) obstacles when carrying out that other well-known British pastime: cycling.

To its credit, Chicago is routinely mentioned among the most cycle-friendly cities in the nation and with its numerous cycle lanes, pay-per-ride Divvy bikes, and the Lakeshore cycling route, it's easy to see why.

But as autumn turns to winter, and as the temperatures plummet and the snow does likewise, it soon becomes unacceptable to simply throw on some loafers and take the old wheels for a spin; there are new rules to consider and new dress codes by which to abide; treacherous roads to navigate and Arctic temperatures to overcome. This doesn't, by the way, mean you should be deterred. After all, as a pro cyclist friend of mine recently advised, "weather is an excuse—not a reason—to stay home." It just means you should familiarise yourself with some of the more well-known survival tactics, such as…

Wrapping Up Warm

In most parts of the UK, the average (and even below-average) cyclist can probably justify adorning themselves in just one pair of each of the following: trousers (pants), socks, underpants (boxers), and gloves. Additionally, a simple scarf, jumper, winter coat, and cycling helmet will usually suffice.

In Chicago, you'll need to double up on everything: under your trousers, wear something flexible, such as a pair of Lycra cycling pants. This might make you feel like the protagonist in a bad 1980s superhero movie, but the extra layer will ensure continued leg warmth. Similarly, two extra pairs of gloves—or a single, highly insulated pair—will go a long way toward persuading your hands not to give up on life, something that they're prone to do when the wind chill is -15°F! It is for this very reason, in fact, that the following garment is not only a nice addition to your winter wardrobe but an essential one: a balaclava. A balaclava—for those of you not familiar with the term (Americans)—is a face mask. Not only does it prevent your face from falling off, but also negates the need for that other accessory—the one that makes you look like Princess Leia: ear muffs.

In addition to the aforementioned essentials, be sure to surround your feet with thermal socks and a solid pair of winter shoes, as well as doubling up on shirts and jumpers (sweaters). Essentially what you're going for is an insulated-but-flexible attire, one that not only keeps you warm but affords you the agility with which to navigate wintry conditions. And speaking of which…

Keep An Eye on Weather Reports

Before heading out the front door like a biker on a mission, be sure to look up weather reports for the Chicagoland area. All might seem quiet on the Midwestern front, but looks—as I've occasionally found to my chagrin—can be deceiving. One minute, the city might be enveloped under a sky of perfect blue, only for grey (gray) clouds to rear their ugly head fifteen minutes after you set off.

Moreover, there is another feature of the winter climate that is arguably more treacherous than the snow. Before heading out, be sure that roads and cycle lanes are devoid of ice. After all, not even your triple layers will act as a safety net for your fibula. That said if you really must traverse the streets during such slippery conditions, consider the life-hack method of repurposing zip ties around your tyres (tires).

Ice, of course, persists longer when the temperatures border on the ungodly. While some would argue that "it all feels the same" once temperatures fall under the freezing point of water, I've never found this to be true. I'd take the unforgivable (and often unforgivingly) bitter grip of a 20°F morning over the barbarous—nay murderous—reality that is single-digit weather. I don't even want to talk about what happens below that. What I do want to talk about—and for your safety—is that, no matter what numbers are showing up on your weather app, remember to occasionally subtract 10 degrees. This is because of wind chill. Wind chill is precisely why the above-named clothing accessories exist. And why mulled wine is a thing.

Speaking of the finer things in life, one good reason to get your wheels out during the months of January and February is that Chicago is beautiful. Sure, those 1970s-era skyscrapers—so dominant across the city skyline—might lean on the wrong side of drab, but navigating the Lakeshore trail, with its snow-covered trees, is something all cyclists should have the good fortune to experience in their lifetime.

Even if you take the city's aesthetic out of the equation, winter cycling—despite the odds—is simply a joy to behold as is. If you follow both the advice in this column and the rules of the road, navigating the brutal conditions of Chicago can be an exhilarating and liberating experience. You just have to see it for the adventure that it is, rather than the drudgery that it is not. You have to think like that protagonist in the bad 1980s superhero movie, refusing to take no for an answer and striving to conquer the enemy as if your badly-dressed life depended on it.

After all, as a wise person once said, the weather is an excuse to stay inside, not a reason.

Laurence is a British writer and humorist who lives in the United States. He also hosts the popular web series, Lost in the Pond on YouTube. He has an infuriating habit of taking America to task by pointing out how things are done in the UK. He really needs to stop this behavio(u)r. It's anti-American.

ALFRED THE GREAT
KING OF WESSEX

Statue of Alfred the Great at Shaftesbury Abbey Ruins

On the year of his death in 899 Alfred the Great was known only as Alfred, King of Wessex. During the first year of his reign alone, King Alfred fought nine bloody battles with Viking invaders, but it was peace, not war, at which King Alfred really excelled. Uniting what was previously a smattering of warring kingdoms, King Alfred started the ball rolling on the eventual unification of Anglo-Saxon England into one nation. A mighty warrior-King and gifted military strategist who introduced the first judicial system in England and taught himself to read, King Alfred was fully deserving of his posthumous sobriquet 'the Great.'

Alfred the Great was not known as 'the Great' during his lifetime, and so little is known about Alfred's appearance that a statue of him in Wantage, Berkshire was given the face of a local Victorian at the time is was made. So, what do we know about the King of Wessex who lived more than 1,100 years ago?

We know that when Alfred ascended to the throne of England, he was not technically the next in line. Alfred's brother, King Aethelred had two surviving children when he died, but in the year 871 Viking aggressors from Denmark were waging war in Wessex and Aethelred's children were neither old enough or experienced enough to take control of the country during a time of war.

Alfred stepped in, and in the first year of his reign, Alfred was forced to prove himself to be a true warrior in no less than nine major battles with Viking forces. The Vikings already had a hold on England as they had been raiding English lands, mostly in the north, since the 790s and had developed permanent settlements in York in the southern part of Northumbria. In the late 800s, the Vikings boldly occupied East Anglia and Mercia and set their sights on taking Wessex. By the tender age of 21, King Alfred was already a battle-weary war vet, desperately trying to maintain armed resistance to the Vikings in southern England.

In 878 the Vikings, led by King Guthrum, seized Chippenham and from there devastated Wessex. The king withdrew to the Somerset marshes to plan his next move. Adopting the Viking strategy of building a fortified base [at Athelney] from which to attack, King Alfred summoned an army from the local area and in May 878, against all the odds, defeated the Vikings at the Battle of Edington.

The victory was not absolute, and King Alfred

Key Facts

- Alfred the Great was born in 849 at the Royal Palace, Wannating, Berkshire now Wantage, Oxfordshire.
- He succeeded as King of Wessex in 871, aged 22. During his reign, Alfred was also declared King of the Saxons.
- Alfred married Ealhswith in the year 868. She survived him and died around the year 902.
- Alfred died on October 26th 899, aged 50. He reigned for 28 years.

knew that he did not have the power to drive the Vikings out of the rest of England. In order to bring peace to his kingdom, Alfred insisted that the defeated Danish King Guthrum receive baptism into Christianity. Shrewd King Alfred knew that a shared religion was the most effective way to unite the native English people with the Viking invaders and hoped that a Christian King would ensure the natives of Danish-occupied Mercia and Northumbria would be spared any violent reprisals.

After the Battle of Edington many Danish soldiers retired to East Anglia where they became farmers. King Alfred conscripted the man-power of Wessex and organized a dual-duty system where men took turns looking after agriculture and defense. Alfred also oversaw the building of a chain of fortified towns across southern England. These well-defended settlements were populated by willing settlers who agreed to defend Wessex in return for their plot of land so that it could never again fall to an invading enemy. Organised around Alfred's palace in Winchester, this network of settlements with strong points on the main river routes ensured that no part of Wessex was more than 20 miles from Alfred's military might. As well as this major building project, Alfred created a royal navy as a new reserve against the sea-power of the Danish.

To consolidate his native alliances Alfred married Ealhswith, a Mercian noblewoman and married one of his daughters, Aethelflaed to the Ealdorman of Mercia. In his private life - as much as he was able to have one in this time of relentless warfare - Alfred was thought to have suffered from some sort of psychosomatic illness. Afflicted with self-doubt, Alfred was regularly

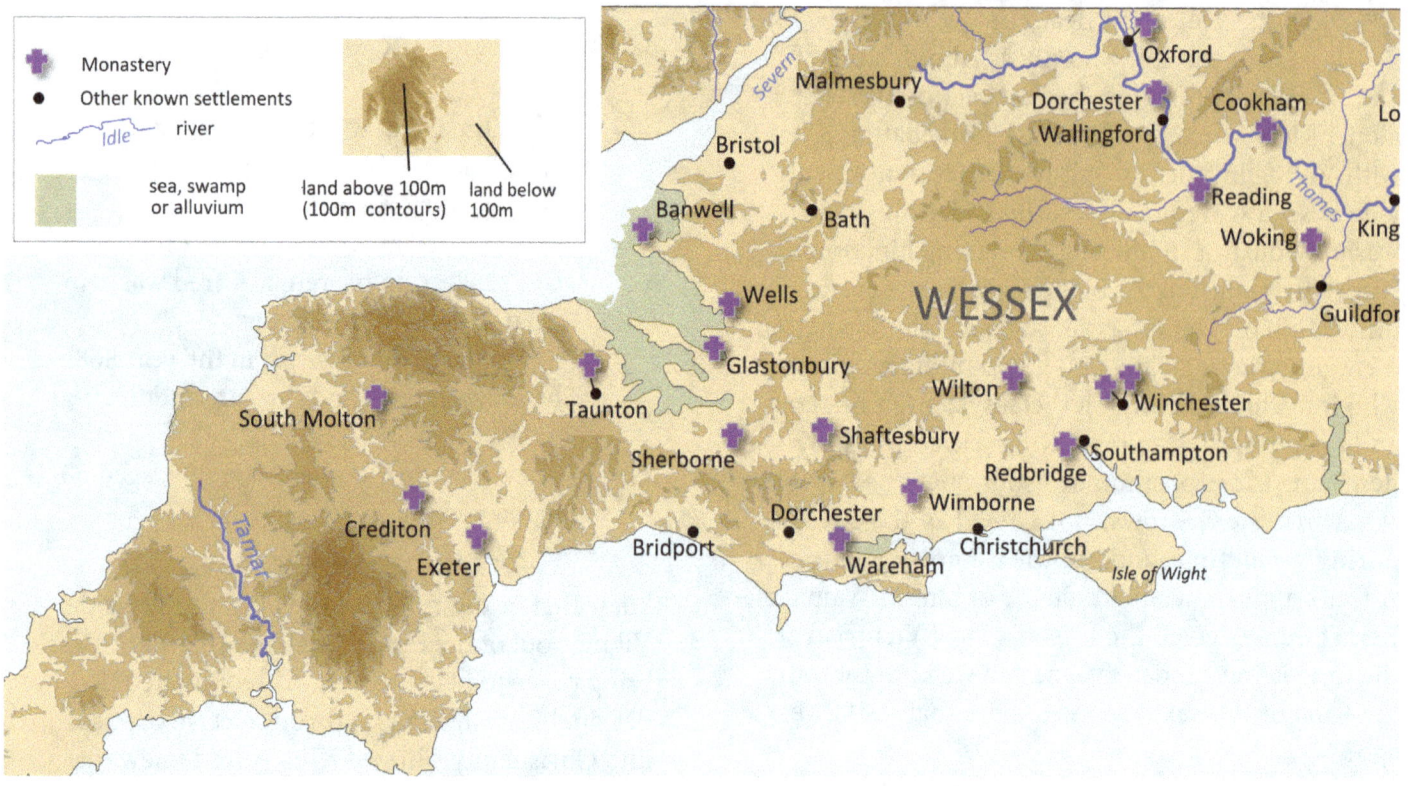

Map of Anglo-Saxon Wessex

Alfred the Great

physically incapacitated during times of crisis and is said to have been humiliated by the fact that he was illiterate. Illiteracy was common amongst even the sons of Kings at the time, and yet Alfred was incredibly ashamed of his disadvantage and eventually taught himself to read at the age of 38.

Despite Alfred's military wins, the major achievement of his reign came in the uneasy years of peace following his defeat of the Danes. Alfred effectively dissolved the insularity of Saxon England by establishing a much-needed judicial system. Studying the best practice of foreign neighbors, Alfred introduced a new code of thoughtful laws that united the Anglo-Saxon kingdoms in common justice.

Alfred also instigated a cult of broad education, using his literacy to give the English people a shared understanding of history and philosophy. Overseeing the translation of a handful of books from Latin to Anglo-Saxon and creating the Anglo-Saxon Chronicle, a patriotic history of the English written in celebration of Alfred and his monarchy, Alfred created a unified and stable kingdom with a strong sense of identity.

Alfred died on 26 October 899 from an unknown illness, but it is thought that the King may have suffered from something similar to Crohn's disease for most of his life. He was succeeded by his son Edward the Elder.

Winchester Cathedral

Legacy Today

Alfred's ultimate achievement was the consolidation of England as a nation. Under assault from Viking invaders, the native people of England were already developing a sense of identity that Alfred helped to cement with his victory over the Vikings at the Battle of Edington. Securing peace with the Vikings, Alfred was able to make major reforms in the reconstruction of Wessex. Alfred created a judicial system and sought to educate the populace of England with the aim of creating a consolidated nation. Although never crowned the King of all of England, Alfred was the King of the Anglo-Saxons and is now known as 'the Great.'

Film and TV

- "Alfred the Great" (1969)
- "Hitchcock: Alfred the Great" (1994) TV Movie
- "The Search for Alfred the Great" (2014) TV Movie
- "The Last Kingdom" (2015) TV series

Further Research

- Merkle, Benjamin (2009). *The White Horse King: The Life of Alfred the Great.*
- Pollard, Justin (2006) *Alfred the Great*
- Simon Keynes (2004) *Alfred the Great: Asser's Life of King Alfred and Other* Contemporary Sources
- Abbels, Richard (1998) *Alfred the Great: War, Kingship and Culture in Anglo-Saxon England*
- Bernard Cromwell, *The Saxon Stories* (fiction)

Locations to Visit

- There are statues of Alfred the Great located in Pewsey, Wantage Market Place, and Winchester.
- In Winchester, visitors can take part in a self-guided King Alfred trail that includes Hyde Abbey Garden, Alfred's last known burial ground.
- Winchester City Museum believes they may be in possession of some of Alfred the Great's remains. This remains unproven, and the bones are not yet on public display.

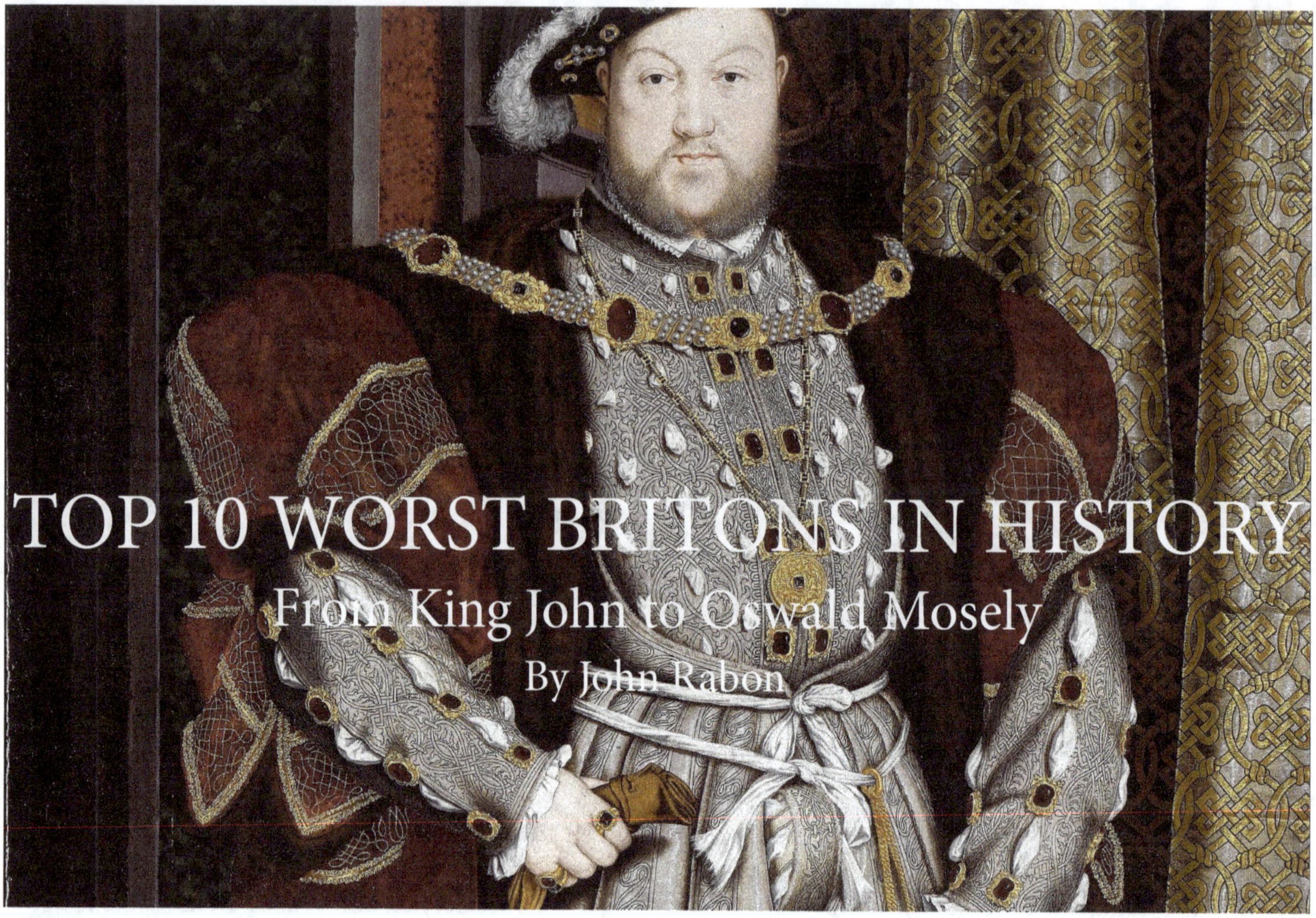

TOP 10 WORST BRITONS IN HISTORY
From King John to Oswald Mosely
By John Rabon

There have been plenty of terrible Britons over time. They robbed, cheated, and murdered. They've committed such heinous crimes that they've gone down in the history books as not only the most horrible people in the UK but the world as well. But who are the worst of the worst? What 10 people belong on this list the most? Of course, this list is only my opinion and they appear in no particular order.

King John

Quite possibly the least popular man who ever sat the throne of England, he was already doomed when he had a hard act to follow in his brother Richard. Like his brother, he continued to fight wars but was far less successful, leading him to raise taxes on the nobility to such an extent that his barons rebelled and forced the Magna Carta on him. John promptly broke the charter as soon as it suited him and had to be forced into it again. It's probably a good thing for him that he died of illness before someone killed him.

Guy Fawkes

The most infamous member of the Gunpowder Plot, Fawkes was part of a group of Catholics who apparently felt King James I wasn't Catholic enough for their liking (due in part to his conversion to Protestantism and subsequent persecution of Catholics in Britain). They decided to blow him and the rest of Parliament to bits, but an ill-conceived letter got everyone caught, with Fawkes being the first arrested. While several more people were involved in the plot, Fawkes being the one caught with the powder made him history's scapegoat to be burned in effigy every 5 November.

Queen Mary I

'Bloody Mary' earned her terrible nickname after she took the throne by force when her brother, King Edward VI, chose Lady Jane Gray to succeed him. Since Mary didn't agree with King Henry VIII's break from the Catholic Church, she opted to undo everything he'd accomplished, ruthlessly suppressing any Protestants who defied her. She further complicated matters for Britons by marrying King Phillip II of Spain, giving rise to a belief that Spain and the Pope would be in full control of England. Mary's foreign and domestic policies were utter disasters, making her even more unpopular.

Thomas Beckett

Certainly, a controversial choice for the list, though historians have argued that a number of the problems during King Henry II's reign were a result of Beckett's actions as Archbishop of Canterbury. The carefree courtier he was under Henry gave way to a man who was a very autocratic Church figure and split English society by siding with Pope Alexander II over Henry, moving to make sure the Church did not have to answer to civil authorities. There are also rumours that he misused the court's funds when he served under Henry and was even put on trial for embezzlement, though it was never proven. Some actually see his assassination by Henry's knights as Beckett's just desserts.

Oliver Cromwell

While King Charles I may not have been the best ruler, his time on the throne was relatively tame compared to the tyrannical control of Cromwell's Commonwealth and the later Protectorate. Under his leadership, Parliament issued some incredibly Puritanical rule, virtually banning leisure on Sunday (except walking to church) and seizing any feasts prepared for Christmas. What's more, he led a very bloody campaign against Ireland that resulted in his troops massacring a village of 2,000 people. It's not much of a wonder that people were more than happy for King Charles II to come back and reclaim the throne not too long after Cromwell's death.

Jack the Ripper

Perhaps the most notorious killer in British history, the Ripper earns the distinction of having never been caught. His six canonical murders (with possibly more tied to him) have gone down as one of Britain's greatest mysteries. Despite Scotland Yard utilising several new police methods to capture him (including crime scene photography, bloodhounds, and psychological profiling), no murderer was ever uncovered. It also wasn't just the number of murder the Ripper committed, but the other savagery and skill by which he sliced up the six Whitechapel women and even removed their organs.

Henry VIII

While King Henry VIII's breaking from the Catholic Church was one of the seminal moments in British history, his Dissolution of the Monasteries was a particularly violent affair that resulted in the deaths of many loyal Catholics and the seizure of Church assets. Then there's Henry's violent temper and his tactic of divorcing or executing his wives on trumped up charges for failing to give him a son. Henry's actions had negative ramifications for decades after his rule ended, and it was only during his daughter Elizabeth's time on the throne that everything settled down and Britain experienced a golden age.

Oswald Mosley

In these modern times, it becomes much easier to understand how a populist spewing hate speech can gain such public attention. Mosley was originally a Conservative member of Parliament before founding the British Union of Fascists after meeting Benito Mussolini. Mosley's protectionist economic proposals were popular with many, but they came with a heavy dose of anti-Semitism. He and his party followers caused several major riots, which resulted in him being banned from the 1934 election and even more violent riots following his marches into Jewish neighbourhoods in 1940. Historians consider Mosley the founder for many modern far-right groups and his influence remains to be seen in the present day.

Duke of Cumberland

Prince William, the Duke of Cumberland and son of King George II, is a particularly nasty villain if you're Scottish. The leading general of the time, William was put in charge of quelling the revolt of forces loyal to Charles Edward Stuart, what is known in history as the Jacobite Uprising. William was a little too eager in his job, famously issued an order of "no quarter" against the Highlanders, even going so far as to punish his officers who showed them mercy. He labeled the rebels as "inhuman savages" and dispensed with any pretense of war etiquette, attempting a genocide of the Highlanders and effectively destroying the clan system in Scotland.

Neville Chamberlain

As Prime Minister before World War II, Neville Chamberlain has become the symbol of appeasement towards Adolf Hitler. Before the war, he negotiated trade treaties with the Republic of Ireland that harmed Britain's economy and later war efforts. Chamberlain was one of those who believed that giving into some of the Nazi leaders demands would help create a stable Europe when in actuality, it played into Hitler's plans to conquer the continent. Chamberlain's conciliations merely emboldened Hitler and ultimately led to his invasion of Poland in 1939 and the beginning of World War II. Chamberlain was judged ill-suited to run the war by Parliament and was replaced with Winston Churchill.

The Armada Portrait - Drake Version

The Armada Portrait of Elizabeth I of England is the name of any of three surviving versions of an allegorical panel painting depicting the Tudor queen surrounded by symbols of imperial majesty against a backdrop representing the defeat of the Spanish Armada in 1588. This particular version belonged to the family of Sir Francis Drake. One of the definitive representations of the English Renaissance, encapsulating the creativity, ideals, and ambitions of the Elizabethan era, it has been the inspiration for countless portrayals of Elizabeth I in film or on stage, and a staple in school textbooks. A public appeal last year was launched to save the painting for the nation, funds were raised successfully, and the portrait is now on display at the recently refurbished Queen's House in Greenwich. Two other versions exist on display at Woburn Abbey and the National Portrait Gallery in London.

GREAT BRITISH ICONS
The Spitfire: A Brief History
By David Goodfellow

© Keith Tarrier / Adobestock

There are few things that instantly evoke the dark days of World War II like the sight of a Spitfire flying through the air, its sleek body cutting the air like a knife, the roar of its Merlin Engines filling the air with an unforgettable noise. It's often been said that the Battle of Britain could not have been won without the Spitfire. And that victory turned it into an icon of the age that has been popular ever since. Its spirit has lived on in films and popular culture to the point where every British child knows what a Spitfire is.

The Spitfire was a fighter aircraft developed in the 1930' by the designer R. J. Mitchell. Revolutionary for the time, this fast, maneuverable aircraft blunted the German air attack in 1940 and gave Britain the breathing space it needed to arm itself to ultimately win, with its Allies, WWII. The aircraft was propeller-driven, with a single wing, marking a departure from biplanes. It had wing-mounted machine guns and later rockets, and underwent continuous improvements during the war, a key to its ongoing success. Fifty-five airworthy planes are still in existence, and numerous grounded planes, along with replicas, can be found around the world. This iconic plane has become a symbol of determination in the face of adversity and overwhelming odds.

On the 16 August, 1940, Winston Churchill, the British Prime Minister, visited the Operational Centre of the Royal Air Force at Uxbridge. So moved was he by the experience that he could not speak for a few minutes. Then he said, "Never in the history of mankind has so much been owed by so many to so few." With 'history of mankind' changed to 'field of human conflict,' this line became the keynote in a speech he gave in Parliament later that month.

"The few" he was referring to were the pilots of the RAF. Since the declaration of war with Germany on 3 September 1939, Poland, Holland, Belgium, Norway, and France had fallen to the Nazis. A British landing force had been repulsed at Dunkirk. The British Navy had barely escaped significant damage at Scapa Flow. Food was rationed because of U-boat attacks on merchant shipping. And for the first time in British history, bombs were raining down on military and civilian targets from the planes of the dreaded Luftwaffe. The United States had declared neutrality in the conflict.

An invasion of England was imminent, and if every Britain needed help, this was the time. That

Key Facts

- Developed in the 1930s in anticipation of the German threat
- Instrumental in preventing a rapid invasion of Britain during WWII
- Allowed Britain to defeat the German Luftwaffe and ultimately win the war
- Iconic and instantly recognisable image of British determination and survival

help came from Reginald J. Mitchell. An engineer, Mitchell had joined the Submarine Aviation Works in 1917. Submarine made sea-planes, and the 23-year-old Mitchell was quickly promoted to Chief Designer, so apparent was his talent. His planes captured prestigious racing trophies and broke multiple speed records. The Air Ministry became involved with Submarine and in 1933 invited Mitchell to design a new fighter plane to replace the aging Air Force biplanes. Submarine Aviation was by this time owned by Vickers-Armstrong.

The first plane Mitchell designed was the Submarine Type 224, but he and his team of designers were not happy with it and quickly moved on to develop and refine the design. The improved plane had an enclosed cockpit with oxygen supply for the pilot, allowing the plane to fly higher, and a retractable undercarriage. It had a small, thin, single wing to reduce drag, developed by Beverly Shenstone, a young Canadian aerodynamic engineer, and a powerful Rolls-Royce PV-XII V-12 engine, which became known as the 'Merlin.' With Air Ministry funding a prototype was built and on 3 January, 1933, a contract was signed for a plane called the F 10/35. The armaments were beefed up from two to four, and later eight, wing-mounted machine guns and the first test flight took place 5 March, 1936. At the controls was Captain Joseph "Mutt" Summers, and the test took place at Eastleigh Aerodrome, which was later to become Southampton Airport. When he landed after the eight-minute flight, Summers was so impressed he apparently said, "Don't touch anything."

Summers' early enthusiasm waned a little, and modifications were made, chiefly to improve the speed to a then very impressive 348 mph. In fact, during a controlled dive the plane reached Mach 0.9,

just below the speed of sound, before the propeller broke up. On 3 June, 1936, the Air Ministry placed an order for 310 planes. Early in its development, the managing director of Vickers had dubbed the plane 'Spitfire,' and the name stuck, although all the various versions of the plane have official titles too. That first contract called for five planes to be produced per week and had a total value of £1.395 million, making each plane worth £4,500 – around $300,000 today, certainly a bargain.

Throughout this time, Mitchell was a sick man. He had been operated on in 1933 for abdominal cancer and never fully recovered from the surgery. Despite this, he carried on working, although increasing his collaborator and ultimate successor, Joseph Smith, was doing most of it. Mitchell died in June 1937, having seen his plane in the air, but unaware of its future role in British history. However, he had travelled to Germany in 1934 and was well aware of the need for Britain to develop a plane capable of withstanding the Luftwaffe. Mitchell was just 42 when he died.

When the air war broke out over Britain, the Spitfire was at the forefront and quickly earned the grudging admiration of the Luftwaffe. When the German ace pilot Adolf Galland was asked by Hermann Goering what he would most like to defeat the RAF, he replied, "Give me a squadron of Spitfires." Although German air-raids continued for much of the war, the ability to fight back and bring down German bombers prevented the rapid conquest that Hitler needed to give him control of Britain, which in turn allowed time for America to be drawn into the war and ultimately gave the victory to the Allies.

The Mark I Spitfire did most of the work during the Battle of Britain, but Mark II planes were already in production by that time and the secret of the success of the Spitfire perhaps lay in the continuous improvements Joseph Smith made to the design, increasing the speed, range, maneuverability, and firepower of the plane. By 1947, 22,000 had been built, with at least 46 variations, including a series for the Royal Navy dubbed the 'Seafire.' Later planes were more heavily armoured, faster and included under-wing rockets. The plane was also used towards the end of the war by the Soviet Air Force and after the war in the British campaign in Malaya in 1951 against a Communist insurgency. Its versatility made it a useful plane in many different

operating environments.

The plane's pouplarity has given it a lasting legacy. Today there are still more than 50 airworthy Spitfires and more than 200 are on display at musuems. Spitfire flights occur at airshows regularly in the summer throughout Britain. You can even attend a concert called the Battle Proms that features patriotic British music, usually on the grounds of a stately home, capped off with a flyby display by a Spitfire. The popularity of the craft has also led to the creation of the Boultbee Academy, offering qualified pilots a chance to learn how to fly the iconic plane. They're also now rented out regularly for private flights.

Sites to Visit and Further Research

The oldest surviving Spitfire (number 155 in production) can be seen at the Royal Air Force Museum, Cosford, in Shropshire. The museum is open from 10 a.m. to 5 p.m. year-round, and until 6 p.m. from March to October.

There are also two Mark I Spitfires at the Imperial War Museum Duxford, in Cambridgeshire. The museum is open from 10 a.m. to 4 p.m., and until 6 p.m. in summer. It also holds several air shows each year, featuring historic planes in flight. On important anniversarys they've been known to gather together many of the still airworthy Spitfires for one big airshow.

There is a sculpture showing three Spitfires in flight at the roundabout junction (known as Spitfire Island) of the A47 and A452 in Castle Bromwich, Birmingham. This is the location of the Castle Bromwich Aircraft Factory where the majority of wartime Spitfires were produced.

There is a film, "The First of the Few "(known as "Spitfire i"n the US) made in 1942 and starring Leslie Howard as R.J. Mitchell, and David Niven as the test pilot.

The film, "The Battle of Britain" (1969) features sequences of Spitfires in simulated battle.

There is a biography of Mitchell, *R J Mitchell: Schooldays to Spitfire*, by Gordon Mitchell (2006)

Spitfire - the Biography by by Jonathan Glancey (2006) is a great nostalgic look at the plane and its cultural influence.

Spitfire: Portrait of a Legend by by Leo McKinstry (2007) is another great detailed history of the plane's development.

THIS ENGLISH LIFE
In the Bleak Midwinter - Moving to London
By Erin Moore

All Souls Langham Place was packed with parents and bristling with anticipation. Settling in to watch my daughter, Anne, perform with her friends in their winter concert, I scanned the program while Henry, her two-year-old brother, squirmed at my side. The Christmas concerts of my South Florida childhood were more "Frosty the Snowman" than "In the Bleak Midwinter," the hymn Year Twos had been practicing. My, her music teacher is ambitious! Lucky for us, he is also patient. The girls are just six, after all.

"In the bleak midwinter, frosty wind made moan, earth stood hard as iron, water like a stone; snow had fallen, snow on snow, snow on snow, in the bleak midwinter, long ago."

My mind wandered as I listened, to a time before the children were born, to the day my husband, Tom, and I left New York in a driving snowstorm. We had done all of the hard things, or so we thought. Our books and furniture were packed and on their way to a container ship; we had said goodbye to our friends and explained our decision to our families. We'd loved living in New York through our twenties, but we couldn't imagine the next stage of our lives unfolding there. We wondered if London would be a better fit for the family we hoped to have. And, thanks to Tom's dual citizenship, we were finally going. At least, we were trying to. Our 9 p.m. flight would stay grounded at JFK until early the next morning.

I imagined a smooth transition. Both of us were to go on working for the same employers. At the time, I was an editor at Gotham, a division of Penguin Books, and many of my authors were British. I was always looking for the next big British book to publish in the US (knowing that a core faithful of Anglophiles like me would love it). We would move over the weekend and go straight to our new offices on Monday. We'd planned everything to the last detail and were feeling optimistic: What could go wrong?

We woke up in London on our first morning—15 February—to sun and snowdrops. We had left the East coast's bleak midwinter far behind. The temperate climate is one of southern England's best qualities; something is always green and blooming.

Everything felt new and strange. Signs in the street and on the underground took on a double meaning. Though we knew that "Way Out" meant "exit" and "Mind the Gap" meant the gap between the Tube train and the platform, it was hard not to focus on how far we were from home, in a place that would go on feeling foreign to us for a long time. It was exhilarating one moment, and exhausting the next. We could take nothing for granted—not even breakfast.

In our local supermarket, we searched. Where were the eggs? Next to the flour and sugar. Not refrigerated! They don't need to be because the protective membranes haven't been washed away in the cleaning process as they are in the US. You may have to deal with the occasional smudge and feather, but it's worth it for their freshness and bright yellow yolks.

Instead of two kinds of sausage (links and patties), we were confronted by 25 different options. Which would we like? All of them, as it turned out. The sausage discovery process would gain us 10 pounds apiece over the next six months.

We would learn to shop every day, since our refrigerator was the size of a footlocker, with a freezer like a shoebox. We'd have to resign ourselves to eating all the ice cream in one sitting. Later we would do as the British do and buy smaller tubs of ice cream. Bigger isn't always better: Who knew?

We had looked forward to the life-expanding possibilities of our move across the Atlantic, but in those first few months in London, our world contracted as we dealt with all the little details of homemaking. We had to choose a neighborhood to live in, and there's no getting around it: London is huge. Our friends were scattered like breadcrumbs, and we realized we would not get to live near all of them. We chose not to choose, renting as central a place as we could afford while we got to know the city.

We settled in a fourth-floor walk-up in Marylebone. It was a neighborhood on the upswing, and we were excited about being so close to the tourist magnets of the West End, being still practically tourists ourselves. The movers were none too pleased when our shipping container arrived-- with 60 boxes of books. They looked as if they'd just as soon start a bonfire on Wimpole Street as carry them all the way up to the flat, and who could blame them?

Next, we had the fun of replacing every one of our household appliances—from the blender to the iron to the electric toothbrush. The US has completely different electrical standards, voltage, frequency, and plug types to the UK. We discovered the wonder of John Lewis, England's all-purpose, dependable department store (Never Knowingly Undersold!). We also discovered the generosity of their returns policy when I bought the wrong size sheets for our bed (not realizing that an American Queen is closer to an English King than it is to a Double). I didn't figure it out until I'd not only washed the sheets but recycled all their packaging. These are the times that try a customer service professional's soul, but our new best friends at John Lewis were unperturbed.

Once we had made our domestic arrangements, our thoughts turned to social life. We weren't going to sit around eating sausages, finishing one another's sentences along with the ice cream, and watching Jon Stewart on Sky cable every night, tempting though it might be.

One of our first invitations was to a birthday party at the home of an American expat friend. He and his wife had been living here for three years and knew a lot of people. We met a lot of friendly faces that night, but the party might as well have been back in our old neighborhood in New York because everyone there was American. We realised then that it would be possible to miss out on making any British friends at all.

We would later come to understand that while other expats are easy and fun to befriend, they tend to skedaddle after about two years when the contract is up, the transfer notice is handed down, or the novelty wears off. Expat friends will break your heart. Anyway, we had come to make a fresh start, and we needed a strategy. We dubbed it The American Charm Offensive, and it consisted of inviting every nice person we met at work over to our new place. Sometimes it went well and sometimes it didn't. Like Anne's music teacher, we might have been ambitious, but we were also patient. Within about six months, we had some reciprocal invitations and slowly, very slowly, over the next few years, we made British friends.

The house we lived in had three flats on the upper

Photo from our early days in London

floors, and we became close with our downstairs neighbors, Trish and Dan. They were kind enough to introduce us to their family and friends, who broadened our circle considerably. We were brought closer by the vicissitudes of living in a 200+ year old house that had been renovated in a way that could best be termed 'casual'. At various times, hastily rigged sewage pipes burst in the living room, the house fire alarm brought everyone to the ground floor in pajamas in the middle of the night, and the lights went out without warning or explanation. One morning, Trish and Dan suffered a close call when their bedroom ceiling fell onto their bed while they were making coffee in the next room--a pile of wet newspaper and horsehair that could have flattened them both.

Office life was a whole new experience. I was most impressed by the non-hierarchical tea getting at Penguin UK. Anyone headed for the office kitchen—regardless of seniority—would offer to bring a cup of tea for whoever else was around. In the New York office, coffee runs were the locus of great snobbery and always delegated to the intern or assistant, a role each of us had taken for a couple of years and then gratefully relinquished. But beyond that refreshing difference, London office politics were a dog whistle. No one could explain it to me—I would have many awkward moments. Like showing up for the company picnic—which was rained out, of course—with a try-hard array of home baked treats wrapped in pretty paper and tied up with bows. Everyone else brought wine. I skipped the pub one evening to go to the gym—not realising that so many important discussions, decisions, and relationships were actually happening there and not in the meetings I dutifully attended (where I'd inevitably say the wrong thing without realising it).

As an editor, words had always been my power and glory, but suddenly it seemed I never had the right ones. The British idiom and slang I was learning felt awkward to use. I decided to double down on my American accent and words, but sometimes they got me into trouble. (Who knew that saying you "quite liked" someone's new project was considered an insult?!)

I would become so curious about these differences in language and culture that I would end up writing a book about them. As Philip Roth once said, "Nothing bad can happen to a writer. Everything is material." But what I remember about my early days in London is feeling so foreign all the time. Sometimes I wondered if we had made a huge mistake. I liked England to visit, but would it ever feel like home? In *This English Life*, I look forward to sharing some of the funny stories, surprising insights, and cultural baggage we have accumulated over here.

We have made many mistakes, but happily, London was not one of them. Ten years later, crowded in among friends and our singing children and a thriving community of like-minded souls, midwinter feels anything but bleak. Tom told me he spotted the first snowdrop flower coming up in the garden just the other day.

About the Author

Erin Moore is an American who has been living in London for 10 years. Her book, That's Not English: Britishisms, Americanisms and What Our English Says About Us, is available on amazon.com.

GREAT BRITISH QUESTIONS

Your burning questions about Britain answered truthfully.

By The Anonymous Anglophile

I have a several hour layover at London Heathrow. Can I explore London or England at all while I wait?

This is a good question. The answer is: It depends. It depends on how many hours you have. If you have more than six hours, then certainly yes. If you're quick about it, go through customs at Heathrow and immediately head for the Heathrow Express. These trains run to London Paddington Station every 15 minutes, and it will deposit you right in central London. You have enough time to take in a museum or a meal. But you must be quick about it. Then hop on the Heathrow Express and head back to the airport. Give yourself plenty of time to get through security - your plane won't wait for you.

If you have fewer than six hours, it's not really enough time to venture into central London. BUT there's still plenty you can do. Heathrow is practically right next door to the lovely town of Windsor, home of Windsor Castle and Legoland (and Eton College across the river). Windsor is a lovely town to wile away a few hours. You can even visit the castle itself; it can easily be seen in a couple of hours. There are plenty of places to eat and soak up some British atmosphere.

Could they skip over Prince Charles after the Queen dies and go right to Prince William?

No, that's not the way it works. We see this constantly in media that the public would prefer Prince William over Prince Charles because William is more popular. A monarchy does not work that way; it's never about popularity. The Crown will pass to Prince Charles the moment Queen Elizabeth II dies (a terrible thought to type out!). Now, being in his 70s now and possibly in his 80s when the terrible event finally happens, he could always abdicate the throne immediately to William. But I doubt that would happen for several reasons. One, he's waited his whole life for the throne. On a personal level, would you abdicate? Second, abdicating in favor of William would require parliamentary approval not just from the British Parliament but from the other 16 countries where the British Monarch is Head of State. It would be a nightmare to fix. Whether the British public likes it or not, Prince Charles will be King and Camilla will be Queen. For how long, now that is the real question. Charles will reign for a few years until old age catches up with him as well and then we'll have a nice long reign with Prince William - he may even reach his own Diamond Jubilee one day!

I want to rent a car on my next trip to Britain, do I need an international driver's license or anything special?

No, you do not need an international driver's license to drive in the UK. Your American License is good for up to one year of driving in the UK. Most UK car rental companies will require you to be over the age of 25 to rent a car, though. We would definitely recommend picking up a copy of the AA Road Manual off Amazon; it will fill you on all of Britain's road rules, which can differ greatly (pro-top: NEVER SPEED, EVER).

What time of year is the best time to travel to England?

Easy answer: anytime of the year. Seriously, we've traveled to England in every month and season of the year, and we've never not enjoyed ourselves. The winter is obviously the least desirable but British winters are much milder than we get in the northern US, so it can actually be quite warm. It's also a lot cheaper. The only downside is that a lot of major attractions are closed. Plan ahead.

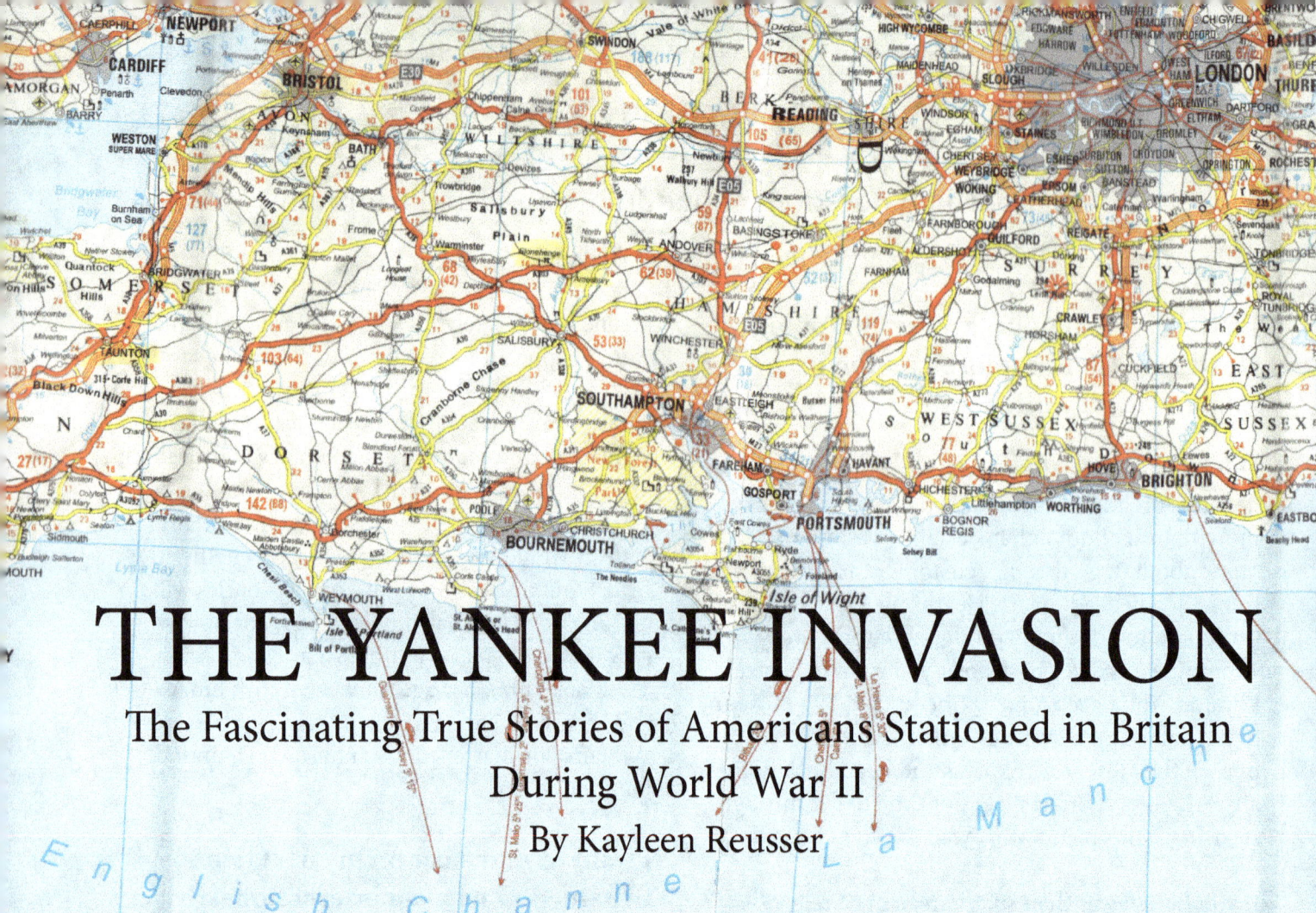

THE YANKEE INVASION
The Fascinating True Stories of Americans Stationed in Britain During World War II
By Kayleen Reusser

The US began fighting against the Nazi regime after Pearl Harbor was attacked on 7 December, 1941. England and other Allied countries in Europe had been fighting Hitler and his oppressive dictators since 1939. American men and women volunteered to serve overseas during World War II. Most had never left their own state. The opportunity to cross the Atlantic to see and live in new places was appealing.

As the American military operated on a 'need to know' basis for information, when GIs (stands for 'government issue') left the US from the East Coast, they had no idea where they were headed. Most headed for the British Isles, landing in Ireland, Scotland, and England.

With America's formidable numbers of troops and supplies, the British people welcomed them with open arms. Though rations were limited all over England, the residents of the great island country offered the best they had to America's military and the Americans reciprocated with hard work and appreciation for the sacrifices the British people had to make.

Though the stories of experiences among the GIs in England are varied, all have a common theme – they were there for a purpose, which was to conquer the evil Hitler and other Axis powers. Together, the people of the US and England made it happen.

Mary 'Polly' Adelaide Woodhull Lipscomb

Mary 'Polly' Adelaide Woodhull was working at a doctor's office in Fort Wayne, Indiana, when Pearl Harbor was bombed. Born in 1913 in Ann Arbor, Michigan, Woodhull had also worked at hospitals in California and Boston before enlisting in the Army Nurse Corps in August 1942.

In November 1942, First Lieutenant Woodhull and other nurses left for England on the Queen Elizabeth, a former luxury ship converted for troops. They arrived two weeks later at the 67th General Hospital in Taunton in southern England, 100 miles west of London. The 67th had been set aside for the recuperation of British, Canadian, and American soldiers wounded in battles, as well as civilians.

Nurses cared for men brought to the hospital by

Left: A map of Southern England provided by Mary

ambulance from the Port of Exmouth.

Soldiers could be operated on and receive good convalescent care and physiotherapy as hospital equipment was excellent. A few wards had steam heat, but most were heated by stoves placed in the middle of the rows of beds.

Since Woodhull had worked in a psychiatric ward in the States, she was assigned to work there. Many patients suffered from what was termed 'shell shock,' or what is today commonly called Post-Traumatic Stress Disorder (PTSD).

Some patients had to be sedated, while others found comfort in doing crafts. The hospital had a loom, and the nurses taught patients how to weave. Some soldiers gave their woven creations to their caretakers. Woodhull kept a placemat and brightly colored orange scarf, gifts from her patients she treasured.

In December 1942 the mayor of Taunton sent invitations to each member of the hospital staff, inviting them to a Christmas reception and dance, hosted by the town's residents. Lipscomb enjoyed the lovely event and kept the mayor's paper invitation as a souvenir.

Still, there were daily reminders that a war was going on. Every Tuesday hospital personnel wore gas masks as part of a drill.

Despite the fear, Woodhull loved living in England, although there were some adjustments. "We ate powdered milk and powdered eggs and had no fresh fruit," she wrote home to her family. "Coffee, which was some sort of chicory stuff, was plentiful and there was tea, but it had a strong taste. We ate dark bread because there was no white flour." Toilet paper was also scarce, as were candy, gum, Life Savers, soap, cigarettes, and canned fruit juice.

The nursing staff never complained about food shortages because the English people endured severe rations. Woodhull thought the English people were friendly, though it was hard to carry conversations as the British accent was hard for the Americans to understand.

Occasionally nurses received time off. Woodhull and girlfriends rode the train to London and were startled to hear air raid sirens. "We followed people to the subway," she said. "It was frightening."

Blackouts were another common war-driven practice. "Every night lights were extinguished

Mary 'Polly' Adelaide Woodhull Lipscomb

throughout London to prevent the enemy from spotting targets," she said. "Many homes had two doors to prevent lights from showing when opened." The blackouts were so effective that people bumped into each other on the street.

The medical staff was not allowed to call home, so Woodhull wrote letters to her family. Shortly after arriving in Taunton in December 1942, she wrote these words in a letter to her parents: "I'm happy to be here to help a little bit for the good old US and the American flag that we Americans are so proud to see over here."

As time passed and homesickness faded, the letters became fewer, especially since Woodhull had a major distraction -- she was in love. The 67th General Hospital had a Medivac ambulance service that transported wounded soldiers across the English Channel. It was a quick way for wounded soldiers to get treatment.

Tech Corporal Alexander Alecston Lipscomb from Oklahoma was a driver assigned to the hospital's motor pool. The two had met at Camp Kilmer before leaving the US and later danced at a USO party in England.

Alec, as he wanted to be called, and Woodhull

Mary On Her Wedding Day

Max Whiteleather

enjoyed each other's company. Being a truck driver, Alec drove her and other nurses back to their barracks at the end of the evening.

The next day, Woodhull was reprimanded by a female officer for disobeying orders. "I knew officers were not allowed to fraternise with enlisted personnel, but I hadn't cared at the dance," she said. "Alec and I continued to meet in movie theaters where it was dark, and people could not see our uniforms to give away our ranks."

By summer 1945, they pair was engaged. They exchanged nuptials at Independent Congregational Chapel, Salisbury Street, County of Dorset on 19 August, 1945. An Army Chaplain conducted the ceremony. The husband of her washer woman from Somerset walked her down the aisle. Only a few friends were present.

Lacking a wedding dress, Woodhull wore her uniform dress blues. "A girlfriend, Margaret Krekler, stood up with me," she said. Alec's best man was his friend Virgil Rust.

The Lipscombs honeymooned a few days along the coast in Torquay; then it was back to work.

Unfortunately, due to Army regulations, they were not allowed to live together as a married couple.

By now, Japan's government had surrendered, meaning the war was over. The Lipscombs looked forward to going home to start their new life together.

One of Polly's final meals in England was an elegant formal dinner created for the officers: Creme Poireaux, Potage St. Louis, Striped Bass Portugaise, Roast Quarters of Lamb with Mint Sauce, and Calf's Head, Grand Mere. The meal was supplemented with vegetables, Fedora pudding and blueberry pie for dessert. "It left a pleasant memory of England's finest with me," she said.

In September 1945, the Lipscombs sailed back to the States together on the *Queen Mary* and were discharged.

They settled in Fort Wayne where Alec became a mechanic. They became parents to three children. Polly resumed her nursing career. After Alec died in 1981, she kept his Army photo in a frame made of British half pennies.

Polly Woodhull Lipscomb's record of military

Vernon Affolder Today

service is recorded at the Veterans History Project. She died 4 June, 10 days prior to her 102nd birthday. The interview from which these stories were taken occurred when she was 101 years old.

Max Whiteleather

In July 1942, Max Whiteleather of Fort Wayne, Indiana, crossed the Atlantic with hundreds of other soldiers on a freighter called the *USS Nightingale*. "It was a 21-day trip," he said. "I was seasick."

The freighter carried 500-pound bombs. In an effort to avoid German subs, the freighter was part of a convoy. "We took the northern route around Nova Scotia," he said. "American ships guarded us half the way; then the British military took over."

The freighter landed safely at Liverpool, England, where the reception was less than joyous. "When British children saw us, they cried in fear because they thought we were Germans," he said.

Not everyone was frightened. A Catholic priest shook Whiteleather's hand. "The priest said we were the first Americans he had ever seen," he said.

The troops unloaded the freighter, then set to work building airstrips on the English landscape. "We built an airstrip every five miles," said Whiteleather. "I never worked any harder than with those Army engineers."

Whiteleather spent the next couple of years in England building airfields. "Every morning we heard Flying Fortresses overhead," he said. The Boeing B-17s received this nickname due to their size as four-engine heavy bombers.

In early June 1944, Whiteleather was part of a massive planned invasion of Allied troops along the French coast of Normandy. Its code name was Operation Overlord; it was more commonly known as 'D-Day.'

"It looked like there were 10 miles of ships," he said. "We could have walked on them to shore."

Max Whiteleather spent the rest of the war moving with Allied forces through other countries. Afterward, he returned to Fort Wayne where he married and became a father to three children.

Whiteleather worked with the railroad for many years. He attended military reunions after the war and participated in Honor Flight of Northeast Indiana 2014, a group that takes World War II vets to Washington DC to see the World War II Memorial and other military monuments.

Vernon Affolder

Staff Sergeant Vernon Affolder of Decatur, Indiana, spent 13 months in Bristol, England, working in the 5th Corps Headquarters. His commander was in charge of all field hospitals and aide stations. Affolder liked record keeping and working with the four officers and six enlisted men assigned to his office.

Affolder enjoyed living among the British. "We learned that if we wanted to find out what the Americans were up to, read the bulletin board in the city park for announcements," he said. "Despite the popular phrase 'Loose lips sink ships' that warned people against talking about the war, we knew if we wanted to know something about the war, ask a Brit!"

Another news source was a female radio broadcaster known as 'BS Betty,' her name reflecting the attitude of the GIs who listened to her. No matter her status as a propagandist, there was no denying her accuracy. "Whatever she announced on

Lewis Harrison Hull and his crew

the radio was usually right!" said Affolder

In June 1944, Affolder's unit traveled to a place in France called Omaha Beach. After surviving there and in the Battle of the Bulge, Affolder returned to Decatur to work at a hardware store before selling life insurance, a career he continued until age 85.

Lewis Harrison Hull

At 12:30 am on 6 June, 1944, Lewis Harrison 'Harry' Hull of Fort Wayne and other flight mechanics were awakened from their bunks at an airbase in eastern England. "We were told to eat breakfast and get the planes ready to fly," he said.

Hull was crew chief of the 61st Squadron for the Eighth Air Force's 56th Fighter Group. The pilots took off before dawn. Hull's job was to make sure their planes were safe and ready.

As a child in the 1920s, Hull had seen planes fly in the sky over his family's farm in northern Indiana. He began to dream of being a pilot. "I told people I wanted to be an airplane driver," he said. "I didn't know the word for pilot."

Unfortunately, Hull failed the color blindness test given to aviator applicants. Undeterred, Hull enlisted in the Army Air Corps, hoping to be a plane mechanic.

After completing plane maintenance school in New Orleans, Hull was assigned to a crew with the Eighth Air Force, 56th Fighter Group in the 61st squadron.

After the bombing of Pearl Harbor in December 1941, Hull was sent to England to work on P-47s at air bases near the villages of Peterborough, Colchester, and Boxsted. "The letter 'P' stood for pursuit," he said. In May 1942, the Army Air Corps pursuit groups were redesignated 'fighter' groups.

Hull hung bombs on the planes and made sure the machine guns worked. "The mission of our crews was to bomb factories and strafe airports, cities, buildings," he said.

Hull's eye for detail in caring for aircraft was quickly noticed, and he was promoted to crew chief. "I never let a plane leave the ground if something was wrong," he said. "When pilots from other squadrons took off, they sometimes had to abort flights because of problems with the planes. My pilots never had to abort."

One time a P-47 pilot was shot down over enemy territory. No body was found, and it was believed the pilot died in the explosion.

After the war, Hull was thrilled to see the downed pilot at a military reunion. "We greeted each other as brothers," he said. The pilot told Hull he had been thrown clear of the explosion and woken up in a German hospital. He was a POW until the war ended.

Then the pilot said the words Hull had always wondered about, "Sergeant, I want to tell you my plane never flew better than that day!"

Not every pilot returned from missions, and that saddened Hull and the other mechanics. When any member of a flight crew was lost during the invasion at Normandy and the rest of the war, Hull remembered a quote from President Lincoln when he lost an election. "Lincoln said it was like stubbing your toe, but you're too big to cry."

Perhaps to deflect the stress of their work, flight crews assigned humorous names to their planes. Hull's planes were named for Snow White's seven dwarfs. "One pilot wanted to be a doctor, so we named his plane Doc," he said.

In September 1944, Hull worked on C-47s prepped to fly for Operation Market Garden, an invasion to overtake Axis forces in the Netherlands.

Allied troops in the Netherlands had been besieged and were running low on supplies. Special 'belly' fuel tanks hung under the C-47s for longer range missions. Hull's crew didn't fill them with fuel, however. "We filled them with K rations for troops," he said. "Unfortunately, bad weather kept us from dropping them, so we ended up eating the rations."

In summer 1943 America's top scoring fighter ace of WW1, Eddie Rickenbacker, visited Halesworth airbase where Hull was stationed.

The WWI flying ace addressed the personnel at the base. Other notable flying figures who visited the base during the war were Carl Spaatz, head of the Army Air Corps, and a WWII flying ace, Jimmy Doolittle. "Their presence and talks were great for our airmen's morale," said Hull.

The war ended in September 1945, and Staff Sergeant Hull was discharged a month later, after providing maintenance on P-47s in England for three years.

Among the souvenirs Hull brought home from the war was a small plane model made of melted bronze from 50-caliber bullets. Plexiglas on the plane's bottom was taken from the side panel canopy of a downed P-47. "A British soldier started to form it from plane parts," said Hull. "He gave it to me, and I finished it." The model has had a place in Hull's home for more than 70 years.

As a result of his time and experience in England in World War II, Hull worked as a plane mechanic at Smith Field in Fort Wayne and also for Bunge (formerly Central Soya) in Decatur, Indiana. He later earned his commercial, instrument, and multi-engine ratings as a pilot.

"My attitude, not my brain, made me a great crew chief," he said. "I was not the smartest crew chief, but I was careful. I was glad when World War II ended, but I would not trade my experiences for anything."

Further Research

- *GI Brides: The Wartime Girls Who Crossed the Atlantic for Love* by Duncan Barrett and Nuala Calvi
- *Eisenhower's Armies: The American-British Alliance during World War II* by Niall Barr
- *'Overpaid, Oversexed, and over Here': The American GI in World War II Britain* by Juliet Gardiner
- *Rich Relations:: The American Occupation of Britain, 1942-1945* by David Reynolds
- *The G.I.'s: The Americans in Britain, 1942-1945* by Norman Longmate
- "Yanks" (1979) Film Starring Academy Award-winner Vanessa Redgrave and Richard Gere who heat up the screen in this captivating drama that follows American GIs in Britain during the second World War.
- *My Mother and Other Strangers* (2016) - Set during 1943 in the fictional village of Moybeg, on the shores of Lough Neagh, Northern Ireland, the series centres around the Coyne family, and their neighbours, as they come to terms with the influx of thousands of American servicemen of the USAAF Eighth Air Force into their small, rural community.

BRIT BOOK CORNER

Curiocity: In Pursuit of London by Henry Eliot & Matt Lloyd-Rose

This book is a difficult book to define. It's essentially an encyclopedia of random Londoness (it that's a word). The authors have gathered together a mountain of facts about London and arranged them in an A-to-Z format divided into 26 sections. The book comes in at a whopping 450 pages, packaged beautifully in a soft red cover. It's filled with stunning illustrations and uniquely hand-drawn maps of London based on an idea the authors are exploring. It's a stunning word of art in itself. It's dense, packed with thousands of facts and interesting bits about London I guarantee most Londonphiles don't even know. But my favorite part of the book is that it captures the essence of London - its history, dizzying cultures, places and peoples. It's rather amazing that they've managed to succeed in one book but they have and it's beautiful. SRP: $55

London Quiz Book by Mark King

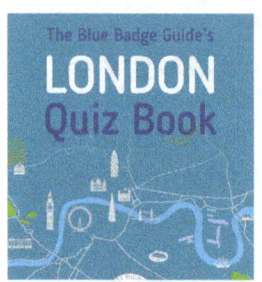

Who doesn't love London trivia? The London Quiz book by Blue Badge Tourist Guide Mark King is a lovely new little move that is exactly what it says on the tin. It features 22 tours of London that feature fascinating questions about London. But King does not simply provide the answer, he also explains it a little more in-depth and provides fascinating context. It's a fun little book and will definitely help you out at your next pub quiz. The History Press SRP: $14.99

Britcoms FAQ by Dave Thompson

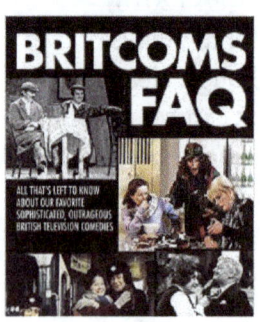

This book is a rather detailed historical look at the history of British comedy aka the Britcom. I'm not sure why the book is called Bitcom FAQ as the book is not laid out like a Frequently Asked Questions book. Instead it explores almost every era of British comedy from the birth of television in 1950s Britain to almost the present day. Sadly, much of the book is focused very much in the past, two-shirts are on comedies that existed before the 1990s and the sections on modern comedy feel somewhat tacked on. British TV has had some of the best comedies every made in the last 15-20 years and I feel these were left out. This book will appeal more to the older audience who would be familiar with the shows talked about in the book - many of which you cannot watch anywhere (as the books talked about thanks to the BBC's history of poor record keeping). So, while it provides tons of great history, many present day Telly fans won't have the faintest idea what some of these shows or who the people involved in them are. If you consider Monty Python the high point of British comedy, then you'll enjoy this book. SRP: $19.99

Churchill's Legacy: Two Speeches To Save the World by Alan Watson

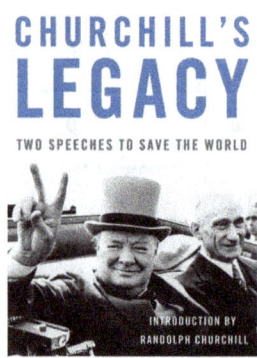

I received this book with great interest as an avowed Churchillian. There seems to have been a rash of books recently about his young life, but this book is different in that it focuses on two key event after World War II and just before he became Prime Minister for the second time. The focus is two speeches. The first is a speech he gave in Fulton, Missouri, where he counted the phrase 'Iron Curtain' in reference to Soviet domination of Eastern Europe The second speech was a few months later in Zurich and called for the creation of a 'United States of Europe' to prevent another European war. Both speeches were controversial at the time, but as with most things Churchill, he was proven to be right after the fact. Watson does a great job of summarising the key events that led to the speeches and the resultant reactions afterwards. It's a short and engaging read - one could read this book in one sitting - and it's an interesting window into the wisdom contained within Winston Churchill, even when he was at a political low point. Bloomsbury SRP $25

The Thames Through Time: A Liquid History by Stephen Croad

In this new release from Batsford, journey along the length of the famed Thames River on a spectacular photographic tour. Spanning almost 150 years gf history, the images in this evocative history include the work of some of the pioneers and leading exponents of topographical and architectural photography. View the rural Thames as it approaches London. See the riverside towns, the working docks and warehouses, the development of the web of bridges that now links north and south, barges, sailing ships and warships, the great flood defenses, the tiny beach that briefly flourished at the Tower of London, and more. Each picture has an interesting caption that puts each in context (and also what happened in the modern era). My favorite contrast we seeing what it looked like before Victoria Embankment was created and after. It's a fascinating trip through London's history that allows you to see it in a different light in beautiful crisp black and white pictures. This book is a wonder of London history and you can almost smell the Victorian squalor in some of the pictures. Batsford SRP $24.95

Great Pubs of London by George Dailey

Brimming with gorgeous photos and witty text, this elegant book celebrates London's most renowned and historic pubs. For centuries the pub has been an essential part of London's cultural and social fabric. This beautifully illustrated book takes readers through the doors of 25 historically and architecturally significant London pubs. Through photographs specially commissioned for this project, readers can explore these institutions from snob screens to 400-hundred-year-old flagstone floors. Engaging texts highlight what makes each pub so special; their place in London's history, the personalities who have frequented them, the events that occurred inside, and the ways pubs have contributed phrases such as "on the wagon" and "one for the road" to the modern lexicon. This book reveals why The Lamb and Flag in Covent Garden earned the nickname the "Bucket of Blood", and features a pub that Charles Dickens described as a "great rambling queer old place". Furthermore, the book muses over the chances that Casanova paid a visit to The Dog and Duck in Soho, and uncovers the location of Charles De Gaulle's favorite wartime watering hole. The book is simply beautiful to behold. The pictures by Charlie Dailey are stunning and each pub is loving photographed. I've definitely come away with a few new pubs to visit on our next trip to London. Prestel SRP $39.95

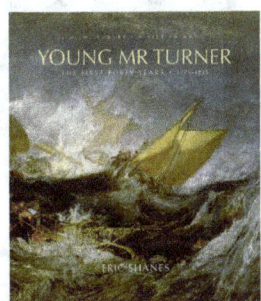

Young Mr Turner by Eric Shanes

The painter JMW Turner has never been more popular (after the hit film starring Timothy Spall as the painter) so it's a great time for a new exploration of his work and life. Young Mr Turner by Eric Shanes, an esteemed academic and Turner expert, explores the first 40 years of Turner's life in great, sometimes not so great detail. Turner was a complex figure, and divisive during his lifetime but he has long been has long been considered Britain's greatest painter. This comprehensive new account of his early life draws together recent scholarship, corrects errors in the existing literature, and presents a wealth of new findings. In doing so, it furnishes a more detailed understanding than ever before of the connections between Turner's life and art. Taking a strictly chronological approach, Eric Shanes addresses Turner's intellectual complexity and depth, his technical virtuosity, his personal contradictions, and his intricate social and cultural relations. There is a lot of detail in this book and as someone who only has a 'Anglophile's interest' in Turner, it is perhaps a bit too much information that I want to know about Turner. That being said, the book is beautiful - massive with hundreds of full color reproductions of his early work and some of his most famous works. It's a wonder to behold and I'm glad to have it in my library. I hope Mr Shanes continues the story with the rest of Turner's life as many of his greatest paintings were in his later years. It's an expensive book but worth every penny. Yale University Press SRP $150

GREAT BRITONS
Exploring the Life of William Herschel

William Herschel began life in the footsteps of his father as a musician and went on to become a successful composer. Then he developed a passion for astronomy and became a founding figure in the modern science of astronomy, making thousands of observations and discovering the true nature of binary stars and nebulae. He discovered the outermost known planet of the solar system at the time, Uranus and the existence of infrared light from the sun. With his sister Caroline, he developed improvements to the telescopes of the time and manufactured hundreds of them by laborious hand methods. His numbering system for nebulae is still in use today.

In the early 18th century, Britain and Hanover shared a king – George II - and movement of people between the two countries was common. It was in this way that the young Friedrich Wilhelm Herschel, who followed his father and brother in becoming an oboe player in the Hanover Military Band, came to Britain – first with the band and then, in 1757, as a 19-year-old refugee from the defeat of Hanover by France in the Seven Years War. The young man quickly learned English and anglicised his name to Frederick William. A skilled musician and composer, he also played violin and harpsichord, and he quickly found work playing and composing, moving from a North-country military band to become the Director of Public Concerts in the fashionable resort town of Bath by the end of 1766. He also played the organ for the Octagon Chapel in that town. His sister and three of his brothers – he had nine siblings in all – joined him in Bath and when he became Director of the Bath Orchestra in 1780, they often joined him on stage. During his life, he composed 24 symphonies, numerous concertos, and some church music as well.

Music and mathematics have a lot in common, so it is perhaps not as surprising as it first seems that when Herschel became acquainted with the Reverend John Michell, an amateur violinist, he should become attracted to Michell's other life, as a forward-thinking natural philosopher interested in astronomy and optics, as well as geography, gravitation, and magnetics. Michell was a remarkable scientist, and he is credited with the first proposal of black holes, the first to recognise that earthquakes travel in waves, the first to invent an artificial magnet, and the first to use statistics to study cosmic bodies. So advanced in fact were his

Key Facts

- Born 1738 – died 1822
- Had two careers – as a musician and composer, and as an astronomer
- Made major discoveries, including binary stars, the planet Uranus, and infrared light
- Built hundreds of telescopes of improved design

ideas that they, and his reputation, languished in obscurity until many of his ideas were re-invented a hundred years later.

When his friend died, Herschel bought one of Michell's telescopes and continued his interest in astronomy, purchasing most of the books available on the subject at the time. He came to know the Royal Astronomer, Nevil Maskelyne, who had worked on the accurate measurement of longitude, a vital navigation tool for the Royal Navy and global exploration. Herschel began to build his own telescope, which at that time involved hand-grinding his own reflecting mirrors – a tedious and very time-consuming task. These mirrors were not made of glass but of speculum metal, an alloy of copper and tin that could be shined to a mirror surface. In this work, he was assisted by his sister, Caroline, who lived with him in Bath and shared his enthusiasm. By 1774, Herschel had developed stricter scientific methods and was keeping a journal of his observations of planets and stars.

His first area of investigation was double stars – two stars very close together – called binary stars. Galileo had suggested that observations of these stars over time could be used to calculate their distance from Earth. When Herschel made the necessary observations and calculations, discovering many new binary stars along the way, he found that they were not what Galileo had thought, just two stars close to each other, but in fact, two stars revolving around each other in mutual orbits. He published his findings in 1803, and his work was not improved on until after his death.

It was during his observations of binary stars that Herschel made the discovery that would make him famous. He observed a new body that was a disk, not a point-source of light, and with the help of the Russian astronomer Anders Johan Lexell, he

William and Caroline Herschel polishing a telescope lens

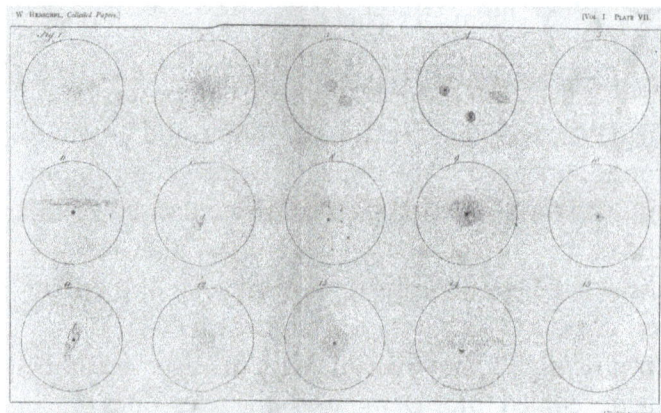

Herschel's Nebulae Drawings

was able to show that it was a new planet, orbiting beyond Saturn. He found favour at the Royal Court by naming the planet 'George III', but this name was not popular in Europe and after some time the consensus settled on 'Uranus' for Herschel's new planet. His discovery earned him the Copley Medal for 'outstanding research' and membership of the Royal Society. He was also appointed 'The King's Astronomer' and moved with Caroline to the village of Datchet, closer to the Royal Court in Windsor.

Over a 20-year period from 1782 to 1802, Herschel systematically scoured the night sky for unusual objects that were not stars. He was the first astronomer to catalogue more than 2,400 such objects, called nebulae, which in the 20th century would come to be recognised as galaxies beyond our own. His catalogues of these objects went through several editions, and his numbering system remains the astronomical standard for nebulae.

In 1783, he gave Caroline, who had worked as his assistant for years, her own telescope and she began to make discoveries in her own right, including nebulae and eight comets. The King started to pay her an annual salary of £50 as Herschel's assistant, making her the first female government employee in British history. All was not, however, goodness and light in the Herschel household, especially when in 1788, he married a widow called Mary Pitt. Caroline was jealous and angry at the loss of her position as head of the household and Herschel's confidant and moved out of the home. In later life, the two women seemed to have resolved their differences and exchanged warm letters. Caroline continued her astronomical work, and in 1828 she was awarded a Gold Medal by the Royal Astronomical Society. Herschel's son John would also go on to become a famous astronomer.

Herschel received numerous awards and memberships, including Foreign Honorary Member of the American Academy of Arts and Sciences in 1788; foreign membership of the Royal Swedish Academy of Sciences in 1813; and he was made Knight of the Royal Guelphic Order, the Hanoverian equivalent of a British Knighthood. He was also instrumental in the founding of the Royal Astronomical Society in 1820.

Herschel made more than 400 telescopes during his life, and his fame and skill enabled him to establish a successful business. He worked on new designs to overcome the limitations of the technology of that period and developed his own design, the Herschelian telescope. His largest telescope had a 49-and-1/2 inch-diameter mirror and a 40-foot focal length.

Compiling observations over many years, Herschel demonstrated a relationship between sunspot activity and climate affecting crop yields; discovered two new moons of Saturn and two of Uranus; demonstrated the fluctuating size of the Martian ice-caps; discovered the disk-shape of

Herschel's 40-foot (12 m) telescope

the Solar System and that it was moving through space, even determining its approximate direction of movement; and introduced the use of the word 'asteroid'. Perhaps his greatest leap forward was the accidental discovery of infrared light from the sun – a discovery that would lead to our understanding of the electromagnetic spectrum. He died at his home on Slough on 25 August 1822.

His Legacy

Herschel developed the groundwork for much of our modern understanding of the universe and established the value of detailed and persistent observation. As the marker on his grave says, he broke through the barriers of the heavens and opened our eyes to the vast nature of space.

Astronomical bodies, from lunar craters to stars, have been named after him and when the European Space Agency sent the world's largest infrared telescope into space, they named it the Herschel Space Observatory. It operated from 2009 to 2013.

Sites to Visit

- Herschel's grave is at St Laurence's Church, Upton, Slough.
- His home in Bath is now the Herschel Museum of Astronomy. Several rooms recreate his life and work. The museum is at 19 New King Street, Bath, and is open during the week from 1 p.m. – 5 p.m. and on weekends and holidays from 11 a.m. – 5 p.m. The museum may be closed in the middle of winter.

Further Research

- *Discoverers of the Universe: William and Caroline Herschel,* by Michael Hoskin
- *The Herschel Chronicle: The Life-Story of William Herschel and his Sister Caroline Herschel,* by Constance A. Lubbock
- *The Georgian Star: How William and Caroline Herschel Revolutionized Our Understanding of the Cosmos,* by Michael Lemonick
- *William Herschel and His Work,* by James Sime

NORTHERN RENNAISSANCE

Exploring Hull: The 2017 UK City of Culture

By John Rabon

The Deep Aquarium © Thomas Arran

Culture may not be the first thing that comes to mind when you think of Hull, but the city is practically bursting with art, music, theatre, poetry, literature, and more. It's got so much culture that it was actually named the UK's City of Culture for 2017 by the Department for Culture, Media, and Sport. The department gives out this prestigious honour every four years to a city that "demonstrate the belief in the transformative power of culture." Cities submit bids for the competition and a panel selects the winner. The winning metropolis then puts on various programmes and performances throughout the year. Hull was chosen because it submitted "the most compelling case based on its theme of 'a city coming out of the shadows.'" But how does such a phrase really describe the City of Hull and what can we expect from it in 2017?

Hull got its start as a port and market town in the Medieval period. The point at which the Humber Estuary and the River Hull joined up proved to be a perfect location to transport goods such as timber to come inland on larger vessels and transfer to smaller ships for shipping further upriver and deeper into England. Hull's port status increased when King Edward I made it a supply base for his wars against Scotland in 1293 and it gained official status in 1299 when Edward granted the city a royal charter as "Kingston-upon-Hull" (or "King's town upon Hull"), which remains Hull's official name.

Hull continued to be an important port city during the English Civil War, as both sides attempted to make use of it for their own ends, though ultimately the city sided with the Parliamentarians. When the Industrial Revolution came along in the next century, Hull prospered even more, and the city also became a prominent whaling port in the last bit of the 18th century, with some 40% of whaling vessels sailing from Hull. Fishing became an important part of the port in the 19th century, and Hull was then granted City status in 1897. Then, as it moved into the 20th century, it bore the brunt of the economic depression and the bombs of World War II.

Even as the fishing industry in Hull rapidly declined in the 1970s, other industries flourished in its wake. Despite the economic problems that the city began to face, exporting and importing were still a major part of the city. Retail and tourism

Humber Bridge

joined the city's ever-expanding business portfolio, with the Quay Shopping Centre opening in 1980 and the Streetlife Museum, Hull's Historic Docks, and the Hull and East Riding Museum joining soon afterward. Hull also started to become a major cultural centre, opening RED Art Gallery in 1997 and Vue Cinema in 2007, joining such venues as Hull Truck Theatre, Hull New Theatre, Hull Arena, and more. And now, as the calendars turn over to 2017, Kingston upon Hull readies itself to become not only a shipping centre but also a cultural hub of the United Kingdom, making each day a celebration of the arts in all its forms.

To manage this honour and establish the programming for Hull City of Culture, the city created the Hull City of Culture 2017 organisation in 2013. Also known as "Hull 2017", it is an "independent company and charitable trust" to work with artists, business, and venues to celebrate Hull's culture and make the city not only a cultural centre of the North, but also a cultural destination for visitors from all over the world. To aid in its endeavour, Hull 2017 has enlisted the aid of more than 4,000 volunteers and formed partnerships with many public and private funding sources, including other corporations and trusts, to meet a fundraising target of £18 million and ensure that the city's calendar is filled with programming. With the combined efforts of the volunteers, fundraisers, partners, and artists, Hull 2017 looks to have at least one event going on every day of the year.

Of course, having something going on for 365 days straight can be a chore for any city, but Hull has it expertly organised from seasons to months to days. The first season, starting (of course) in January is called "Made in Hull" and will be about the spirit, stories, and talent of the city. Opening the event will be a fireworks celebration to rival that of London's New Year's Day extravaganza on 1 January. Then, running from the 1st through the 7th, is an event that combines performance, history, and activity also called "Made in Hull", in which the city's history will be projected in images on the sides of its most famous landmarks to form a walking trail that takes residents and visitors alike on a journey through Hull's most important moments. Additionally, January brings the opening of the Humber Street Gallery and the reopening of Ferens Art Gallery as well an exhibition of Michaelangelo's line drawings at the University of Hull. Hull 2017 CEO Martin Green says that the city will "roar" once all the celebrations get started, and it appears that the company has no plans to slow down.

Hull City of Culture looks to incorporate every aspect of the city into its programming, as evidenced by Made in Hull. More than images on buildings, sound recordings, and public performances, nearly everything in the city from its landmarks to its public transport and the citizens themselves will be involved. Back in July 2016, American photographic artist Spencer Tunick enlisted thousands of Hull residents, covered head-to-toe in various shades of blue body paint, to create his work "The Sea of Hull," which will debut at Ferens Art Gallery. These photos featured everyone stark naked, but for the paint, in the streets of the city to celebrate a relationship with the sea that has provided so much in the way of life and economy. Another example is the "Airbrush Bus," an idea from Hull bus driver and artist Keith Holmes, who airbrushed famous natives and places on the side of his public transport to help teach children and visitors about the city's history.

The "Made in Hull" theme comes to a close after March. Beginning in April, the theme becomes "Roots and Routes," which will focus on Hull's status as a gateway to both the United Kingdom as well as the rest of Europe. Hull 2017 intends for this chapter to "explore our unique place in a constantly changing world" and, as a result, will have a more international theme. From July to September, it's all about "Freedom," and Hull opens itself up to artists who are innovative and rebellious, inviting creative types who like to push boundaries and explore the full meaning of freedom. What's more, Hull will reflect on its own history of freedom with works that honour the life of William Wilberforce, one of the leaders of Britain's abolitionist movement. The final chapter for Hull City of Culture will be "Tell the World," which explores where culture goes from here, not only for the city but the whole of the United Kingdom.

It is the hope of many that Hull City of Culture will change the perception of the city to outsiders and make Hull a major tourist destination. For some, the City of Culture honour will be "an explosion of culture and regeneration in this city [that] has not been seen since the 1950s", according to a BBC interview with Hull City Councillor Stephen Brady. "Our vision was to use the city's heritage and culture to create jobs and to put Hull back on the map as one of the great cities of northern England. That vision is fast becoming a reality." One way in which that vision has already begun to come true is the BBC Director General Tony Hall's promise to feature Hull on every BBC local and national weather map during 2017.

Even with such a ringing endorsement, since the initial announcement from the Department for Culture, Media, and Sport in 2013, the idea of Hull as a City of Culture has met with some criticism from people outside the city and those who live within it. In the past, Hull has been on the receiving end of such unflattering nicknames as "Hell," "Dull," and "Hole"...and that's from its residents. Outsiders voted it as the "Number One Crap Town" in the UK in 2003 and the Economist magazine once described it as an "urban ghost." After the announcement, Hull City AFC fans would chant "You're only here for the culture!" at visiting clubs. Even critics such as BBC Arts Editor Will Gompertz were skeptical about the City of Culture honour's ability to make Hull a destination location.

These attitudes seem to forget the unique place that Hull has had in British history and the development of British culture as a whole. This is a city that was instrumental in the English Civil War by denying King Charles I access to its armory, a moment that forms the basis of The Hypocrite, a play by Hull-born Richard Bean, which will be performed at Hull Truck Theatre. Besides William Wilberforce, Hull counts amongst its famous sons and daughters Phillip Larken, one of England's best poets, who spent more than 30 years working at the Hull Library and will have an exhibit of his works. Anthony Minghella, who studied at the University of Hull and went on to be the director of

Hull City Hall — © Neil Holmes Photography

such award-winning films as The English Patient, The Talented Mr. Ripley, and Cold Mountain, will be the subject of a retrospective.

What's more, the City of Culture is attracting a number of national festivals to Hull for 2017. Festival LGBT will mark its 50th anniversary of the decriminalisation of homosexuality by hosting its events in Hull during July, combining its celebrations with UK Pride and the city's own Pride in Hull annual event. Contains Strong Language, a four-day literary and spoken word festival sponsored by the BBC, opens on National Poetry Day on 28 September, with Hull as its inaugural host. WOW (Women of the World) will have its 2017 festival in Hull during the month of October, bringing its message of gender equality and giving particular attention to Hull-born pianist, composer, and conductor Ethel Leginska, having been a pioneer for women conductors and the first woman to conduct many of the world's symphony orchestras.

Even gentlemen like Mr. Gompertz admit that the City of Culture honour has the potential to transform Hull into something new. For Hull, "coming out of the shadows" means a chance to get out from the economic fallout of the 70s and a reputation of being a boring place, to forge a new identity for itself as a beacon of culture. A spotlight on Hull will bring to attention to its artists and its people, not just those already famous, but those waiting in the wings for their chance to shine. Instead of meeting bemused expressions and questions of "Where's that?", Hull's citizens abroad will hope to find stories of those who have visited their community and left forever changed by the wonderful, artistic experiences had there. By the end of 2017, Hull plans to earn its place on the map.

For Britain, the relatively new honour of the City of Culture is still defining itself. For Hull, being the City of Culture is a chance to redefine itself for Britain and the rest of the world. Together, the two have a momentous opportunity to shape what each other will become and will leave each other forever changed. And while Hull 2017 Board of Trustees Chair Rosie Millard has described Hull as "an unknown city in the UK," CEO Martin Green has said it's in "human nature to discover the unknown." This unknown quality, as Millard pointed out to the Independent, has enabled the city to "forge its own culture" and given it a "different view of the world" as Green described. Next year, as Hull prepares to take its place as the City of Culture, it will share its view, its people, and its culture with the whole of the UK, inviting everyone to discover the unknown and leave enriched by what they find.

LONDON UNCOVERED
EXPLORING HIDDEN LONDON WITH PETER DAZELEY

Library at The Honourable Society of Lincolns Inn

Peter Dazeley has spent a lifetime photographing London's most iconic locations. He's recently released a new book called *London Uncovered* that peels back the curtain on many unique locations in London that tourists don't often see. It's a fantastic followup to his bestseller, *Unseen London*. Peter took some time to answer our questions about his life and work.

The photographer at work

What's your favorite place in London to photograph? So many of the places were a delight to uncover. I particularly love the stunning Grand Staircase of the St Pancras Renaissance Hotel. Also I had great fun photographing the wonderful historic shop - John Lobb Bookmaker, they gave me access to the 'lasts' (shoe moulds) of their deceased clients, and on opening a cupboard I found the lasts of Princess Diana, Jackie Onassis/Kennedy, Frank Sinatra and Duke Ellington! Also when I photographed the Norfolk Cloisters in The Charterhouse I discovered that football's offside and throw in rules were invented to keep Carthusian schoolboys in check. So many stories from these locations and so much to tell.

What type of equipment do you use (for us photo geeks)? I shoot using a Nikon D800, with Nikkor 24 – 70 mm and 14- 24mm lenses, on tripod.

Have you ever been chased out of somewhere you were trying to photograph? No, access is pre-arranged for photography, I was welcomed everywhere as many of the locations were delighted to be included in the book, though in some I had very limited time. There was so much interest in my last book, *Unseen London*, which featured locations that were less accessible and from readers' feedback we discovered that *Unseen London* had stirred up the readers' appetites for more. The readers now wanted a book featuring lesser known locations that are accessible, to explore and discover the locations themselves and bring the book to life. So this latest book *London Uncovered* only features London locations you can visit, but also adds website information on how to visit them too. It is proving a huge hit with visitors to and lovers of London.

What's your least favorite place to photograph? St. Mary Le Bow Church, which houses Bow Bells, was a delight to visit. There is a saying that you are only a true London Cockney if you are born wit'hin earshot of the sound of Bow Bells. Standing in the crypt in the 10th century London church was amazing. To photograph the bells themselves, was fun until they rang right next to my ear. It took me by surprise how loud they were!

Which place is most difficult to photograph? Everywhere has been delightful so I can't say anywhere was difficult to photograph. From a technical point of view, digital photography makes my work so much easier than film, to deal with the mixed and challenging lighting I faced. For the really dark places I use a tripod and long exposures to record the environment faithfully. It has been my privilege to photograph and record my wonderful city as it stands in the 21st century to share with the rest of the world.

Easiest? Cleopatra's needle on the Thames and the Peace Pagoda in Battersea Park. Great monuments with great stories behind them.

Are you working on another book? Yes, I have just completed my third book, *London Theatres*, which features 48 locations. It is being published by Frances Lincoln Oct 2017. It is amazing to see the beauty and variety of theatres in London, some with extraordinary history. The wonderful Sam Wanamaker's theatre is featured which is completely candlelit for its performances, it was a joy to shoot just using the candle light. On the same site beside the Thames is Shakespeare's Globe, which has regular performances.

Our audience is primarily American, which places do you think are a must visit? I would encourage everyone to really get out and walk around London it is a really amazing city with fantastic history. Strolling through the historic shops like James Smiths or going to a show at Wiltons Music hall would be a unique experience. Also a visit to the beautiful Apsley House, at No.1 London would be breathtaking.

St Pancras Renaissance Hotel London Grand Staircase

Apsley House No1 London End View of The Waterloo Gallery

Wilton Music Hall

Eltham Palace The Entrance Hall

St Mary-le-bow Bow Bells Belfry

The Undercroft Lincolns Inn Chapel The Honourable Society of Lincolns Inn

Peter's new book London Uncovered is available from bookstores worldwide. Published by Francis Lincoln. SRP: $50

ALL PHOTOGRAPHS © PETER DAZELEY USED WITH PERMISSION

THE SLANG PAGE
Latest London Street Slang

English is a forever evolving language. It changes the most on the streets of London as the various ethnicities that have settled in London co-mingle their native languages with English. Interesting things result from this. There are new words all the time, old words are brought back into fasion, some words now mean the opposite of what they used to mean. It's all very fascinating and confusing to visitors as well!

Here are a few new words that have made their way into the current London Urban vernacular. Some of them may still have you scratching your head. And the meaning may completely change by tomorrow morning!

Peng - N - Excellent, very good, attractive. Popularised on the streets of London in the ethnic neighborhoods. "She is so Peng." "Or that food was the Pengest munch."

Peak - Adj - One would think this would be an adjective to describe something grand, it actually means the exact opposite. "There's a rail strike again this weekend; it's so peak".

Bossman - N - Used to refer to a shopowner or someone working in the service industry. Like the person serving you chicken at the local chippie. "'Ello Bossman, I'll have four thighs."

Mandem - N - A group of acquaintances that aren't as cool as they think, slightly ropey. "Oh looks like the mandem are hanging out a the skate park again."

Roadman - N - That intimidating, slightly sketchy looking character who knows the neighborhood better than anyone. Probably the person to ask for direction. "What? Does he think he's some kind of roadman?"

Northerner - N - Anyone who lives outside the M25 ring road that surrounds London. "I think he's a Northerner."

Blower - N - The phone. "Hey mate, your dad's on the blower."

Lit - Adj - Something that is exciting or big bash. "Man, that party was lit!"

Dench - Adj - Someone who has bulked themselves up successfully. "You are so dench now that you have been down the gym."

Wavey - Adj - To be drunk or high on drugs. "He was so wavey at the party last night."

In Ends - N - Your local area. "I've been in ends all day, mate."

Link - V - To meet up with friends or hang out. "Don't forget to link up with us later."

Chirpsing - V - Casual flirting. "He was over there chirpsing with the girls."

Choong - N - Good looking, attractive. "Oh man, he was soooo choong."

Tekker - N - Someone with great technical ability. "Hey, take this over to the tekkers down the street to get it fixed."

Vex - Adj - Angry. "I heard her on the phone earlier; she was vex."

Reh teh teh - Adj - A phrase that basically means etc.

Looking criss - Adj - Looking fresh, sharp. "I saw her coming out of the hairdressers and she was looking criss."

Kicks - N - A pair of American style sneakers (normally called trainers in England). "Did you see his beautiful new kicks?"

www.ingramcontent.com/pod-product-compliance
Lightning Source LLC
Chambersburg PA
CBHW050622120526
44589CB00049BC/2715